One Foot on the Rockies

One Foot on the Rockies

Women and Creativity in the Modern American West

Joan M. Jensen

CH

A Volume in the Calvin P. Horn Lectures
in Western History and Culture

University of New Mexico Press
Albuquerque

LIBRARY OF CONGRESS CATALOGING-IN-PUBLICATION DATA

JENSEN, JOAN M.
ONE FOOT ON THE ROCKIES:
WOMEN AND CREATIVITY IN THE MODERN AMERICAN WEST
JOAN M. JENSEN. — 1ST ED.
P. CM. — (CALVIN P. HORN LECTURES IN WESTERN HISTORY AND CULTURE)
INCLUDES INDEX.

CONTENTS

OUT THERE, OUT WEST: CREATION STORIES
AN ENERGY OF THEIR OWN: THE ARTISTS
NAMING A PRICE, FINDING A SPACE: THE MARKETPLACE
THE HUNGRY EYE: AUDIENCES
WITH THESE WORDS: SILENCES/VOICES
FROM THE BORDERLANDS: CREATING A MEMORY

ISBN 0-8263-1596-8 (CLOTH)   ISBN 0-8263-1539-9 (PAPERBACK)

1. FEMINISM AND THE ARTS—SOUTHWEST, NEW. 2. ARTS, AMERICAN-SOUTHWEST, NEW.
3. ARTS, MODERN—20TH CENTURY—SOUTHWEST, NEW.
4. WOMEN ARTISTS—SOUTHWEST, NEW—PSYCHOLOGY.
I. TITLE. II. SERIES.
NX180.F4J46 1995
700'.82—DC20   94-18695
CIP

DESIGNED BY SUE NIEWIAROWSKI

EXCERPTS FROM JUDITH BACA INTERVIEWS (AUGUST 5–6, 1986) BY AMALIA MESA BAINS
REPRINTED BY PERMISSION OF THE ARCHIVES OF AMERICAN ART, SMITHSONIAN INSTITUTION.

EXCERPTS FROM THE INTERVIEW OF SUSAN BILLY BY SANDRA METZLER WITH DOT BROVARNEY
REPRINTED BY PERMISSION OF THE MENDOCINO COUNTY MUSEUM.

EXCERPTS FROM *For Colored Girls Who Have Considered Suicide/When the Rainbow Is Enuf*
BY NTOZAKE SHANGE, © 1975, 1976, 1977 BY NTOZAKE SHANGE,
REPRINTED WITH THE PERMISSION OF MACMILLAN PUBLISHING COMPANY.

EXCERPTS FROM THE LETTERS OF JOHN AND GRACE HUDSON
REPRINTED BY PERMISSION OF THE GRACE HUDSON MUSEUM, UKIAH, CA.

CONTENTS

Preface VII

Introduction 3

Part One

1. Out There, Out West: Creation Stories 15

2. An Energy of Their Own: The Artists 37

3. Naming a Price, Finding a Space: The Marketplace 59

4. The Hungry Eye: Audiences 83

Part Two

5. With These Words: Silences/Voices 107

6. From the Borderlands: Creating a Memory 131

Notes 153

Index 171

PREFACE

This book is the outgrowth of a series of four talks I gave for the Calvin P. Horn Lectures in Western History and Culture at the University of New Mexico in November 1991. After the first talk I had the chance to talk to Calvin Horn about his publishing ventures in western history. I was enormously impressed by his dedication to western history and by his contributions to that history through his many publications as well as his sponsorship of this lecture series. I thank him for that support.

Many other people also helped make possible the Horn Lectures on Women in the Modern West. Dick Etulain invited me to speak on women in the twentieth century West. He did not say which women or which West he had in mind. I know a lot of the new western women's history because I have read much of it and because I am one of a number of historians who wanted to replace the older image of western women of a decade ago—mainly Anglo pioneers and prostitutes—with a new multicultural image, and to rewrite western history with women at the center. Others, not I, have done most of the work in creating this new western women's history, but I suppose Dick thought I would bring some sort of synthesis of this work to the lectures.

I began this research on western women by reading the work not only of historians, but of folklorists, American Studies experts, anthropologists, ethnologists, literary experts, art historians, women's studies scholars, and others. Despite the richness and variety of those works, I still lacked a focus. The more I read about the arts created by western women, the more the women disappeared because I had no single pat-

tern within which they could move. There seemed to be a lot of creative women in the West, but no pattern to explain their lives. At first
I looked for a center around which to create a pattern. Soon I realized
that rather than centering the patterns that were emerging among the
western women I was coming to know, I must strike out in a new direction, allowing a number of patterns to come together without a center
but with many borders.

I thank all those who have worked so creatively to make this new
world of western women visible enough for me to move off in this direction. Many readers will recognize how their own work informs my
own. This written version of the lectures shows more explicitly than
could the lectures how much has been done and how valuable the work
has been to me.

When I first struck out in what seemed to be a new direction, I
encountered people who recklessly urged me along my then inarticu-
late way. When I told David Holtby at the University of New Mexico
Press that I wanted to do something about women and creativity, he
immediately responded in just the way an ideal publisher should. I sus-
pect this enthusiasm is carrying the Press to a place of its own in the
creative history of the Southwest.

I became so intrigued by my vaguely conceived topic of women
and creativity in the twentieth-century West that I could not let go of
it. All the reading I had done; all the paintings, the baskets, the pottery, the novels, the dances I had seen; all the questions I had about the
results I had seen of women's creativity, as well as what I had not seen
but knew must be there took hold of me. I could not shake the subject
and retreat to some more reasonable place. My research strategy was
the most chaotic and haphazard it had ever been. A graduate student
who suggested such a project would be sharply challenged by me for
such formlessness.

Within six months of the lectures I was still aimlessly reading and
worrying about how I would pull this together. Then I saw a notice
from the Women's Studies Program at the University of Arizona about
Rockefeller Fellowships for the summer. I wanted one, which meant I
had to get *something* down on paper. Fortunately, Susan Armitage, Linda
Kerber, and Vera Norwood, all of whom are American Studies experts
as well as historians, thought my formless ideas intriguing enough to
write recommendations. I applied to spend six weeks in the Tucson

heat, and I got one of the fellowships. It gave me weeks at a guest house (with an air conditioner) vacated by a Turkish scholar for the summer, a really excellent library in western culture, helpful librarians and student workers, welcoming friends, and three other fellows (in architectural history, Francophone literature, and Asian-American literature) with whom to enjoy seminars and dinners. I found Thai restaurants, a ready supply of fresh carrot juice, Alejandro's tortillas, and Antigone Bookstore. These, combined with a few weeks spent at the Huntington Library and a few days at archives in Mendocino County in northern California and at the Archives of the Performing Arts in San Francisco, were what I had to go on. Later, as I struggled to expand and revise the lectures for publication, Sue Armitage, Betsy Jameson, Judy Lensink, and copyeditor Anne Gibbons all offered suggestions on how to clarify my ideas. This book is what I came up with. My thanks to all.

ONE FOOT ON THE ROCKIES

INTRODUCTION

"I see America dancing, standing with one foot poised on the highest point of the Rockies," wrote dancer Isadora Duncan in the 1920s. Duncan was echoing Walt Whitman's 1860 poem, "I hear America singing." Sixty years later, rather than singing as they worked, Duncan's Americans danced in the West.[1]

For Duncan, as for many Anglo-Americans, the West represented not just a physical place or series of experiences upon which to ground cultural descriptions, but an escape from the realities of an industrialized East and a racially divided South. When Americans danced for Duncan, they did not move to Jazz rhythms, as in practice many did, but to a mix of European and Indian rhythms. In the West, at least the mythical West, such images could flourish without facing the distressing contradictions of race and class. There a new culture, not dominated by Europe or the East—North or South—could represent what Americans wished to be. This book is concerned with how some twentieth century western women participated in and responded to a West that was all three—a place, an experience, an escape.

"Out There, Out West," the title of the first chapter, is an image held by many easterners of the great suburb of New York stretching westward to their hinterland. That West, of course, does not exist to those who have lived for some time "out there." We are more likely to see the West as a set of dynamic regions and cultures. I have taken the Pacific Southwest as the primary locus of this work. This area has as its outer borders Mexico and the Pacific. Its internal borders are the Pa-

3

cific Northwest and the southern Rockies. Within these borders, I have
cut a swath I call the Southwest fertile crescent.

This crescent is only one part of the Pacific Southwest. It is a space
where patterns of women's creativity emerged most quickly as I began
to imagine how the Pacific and Mexican borderlands might provide a
place of focus for me. The region that I write of as a fertile cultural
crescent begins in Mendocino north of San Francisco, sweeps south
and east through California and Arizona, and then north of Santa Fe
to Taos. My directional locators move north and east rather than west.
This is, quite frankly, all that I could manage of the area so generously
allotted to me by Dick Etulain.

Even this narrow swath presented problems. I started out with a
generally vague wish to look at women of different cultures who had
been creative in the fields of visual, performing, and literary arts, but
their number and spectacular activities confounded me. I did not want
to accept the impossibility of including this cast of literally thousands
in my regional show; nevertheless, I had to choose. Scholars are always
making choices—and always worrying if those choices are politically
as well as intellectually correct. I admit to uncertainty. I expect others
will let me know how well or poorly I have done in my first swing
through this Pacific Southwest cultural crescent.

I have not defined creativity, nor created arbitrary boundaries around
what is and is not art. For the most part, I talk about artists who created
work for the public and the marketplace and whose work was considered important by a large public. I do not talk much about traditional
women's arts, such as quilting or crochet, colcha or gardening, although
I consider these to be art forms in which women have excelled. I have
tried to look at women and creativity in ways that help us put this
creative heritage back together, ways that enable us to see the enormous importance of this work to our lives and cultures.

To create, women needed first to participate in environments that
made further effort worthwhile. They needed at least four essential elements: an ideology that valued their creativity, cultural support that
sustained their creative lives, a market or exchange system that provided a demand for their cultural products, and an audience that understood, criticized, and kept their cultural traditions alive. Men, of
course, needed the same conditions to create. In the twentieth-century
American West, men managed to create these environments more fre-

quently than women and, intentionally as well as unintentionally, excluded most women from them. It may be that women in the West found more acceptance than women in the East, but that question is not my concern here. It is clear that western women have had cultural experiences and a history separate from the men among whom they live. Sometimes that separateness has been embodied in different arts, sometimes in a distinctive content within arts practiced by men and women, and sometimes in a unique voice within an art dominated by men. The artists I discuss in the following pages have participated in all three of these cultural patterns in rich and complicated ways.

Assigning labels to cultural periods is always tricky, for culture is not like politics. Picking a war or a political upheaval to mark political transitions is relatively easy. Cultural change, however, proceeds unevenly. It may move outwardly or inwardly in concentric circles until the last of the old and the first of the new seem to merge, or like creosote bushes or fairy rings change may grow at the edges leaving the center of the circle without growth. Sometimes, change comes like crystals formed in successive rings, moving outward from one small chemical reaction. Like a star, new cultural patterns can form from material already present but brought suddenly together by some external event. When growth takes place at the margins, it may simply move inward and dissolve the center. During periods of transition, as a new center forms, things look fairly chaotic, but the present always seems that way. The trick is to see when that center takes form. I have chosen to divide the cultural history of the twentieth century West into three periods: Postfrontier, 1890 to 1920; Modern, 1920 to 1945; and Postmodern 1945 to the present.

Many historians have labeled the period from 1890 to 1920 as the Progressive Era, a term I have come to consider inadequate because it was coined by small groups of middle-class Anglo-Americans to describe their particular emphasis on a constellation of political, social, and intellectual changes they desired. While progressives and their critique of society extended into the West, it has never quite fit the many changes that occurred there. I was looking for a term that might describe the West but be expanded eastward to the cultures of the entire country.

Yet the term Postfrontier has its problems as well. The "frontier" is embedded in concepts of an expanding nation developed by middle-class Anglo-Americans at the end of the century. Some scholars have argued that "frontier" should refer to a place where cultures come together but the suspicion lingers among scholars attempting to write multicultural history that the term assumes as proper a domination by Anglo-Americans of the cultures of other peoples. Nevertheless, I have adopted the term here for lack of a clearly better one. Concepts of the "West" and the "frontier" were created by nineteenth-century Anglo-Americans to explain their visions of the "other" part of the continent. Once the West was identified as something unique and special, people began a search for a single "western" culture as defined primarily by Anglo-American males. By using the term Postfrontier, I wish to call attention to these thirty years as a time when women of different cultures, with visions of their own, contested the creation of a single western culture dominated by white males.

Modernism has been variously defined as beginning in the fifteenth and sixteenth century, as in "modern western communities"; the late nineteenth century; and the early twentieth. I apply the term *modernism* to the period from 1920 to 1945 (although some of the elements were visible in the arts earlier) because during this period of few opposing cultural paradigms modernism became the mainstream.

Some critics call the period of the 1960s late modernism, but clearly the cultural mainstream was breaking up and re-forming. Arnold J. Toynbee used the term *postmodern* in the 1930s to refer to the period since the late nineteenth century. In 1959 C. Wright Mills described a postmodern epoch. In 1961 Jane Jacobs tolled the death of modernism in *The Death and Life of American Cities* when she attacked urban architecture and what it had done to the lives of urban dwellers. Five years later, in 1966, Robert Venturi described postmodernism without naming it in *Complexity and Contradiction in Architecture*. He denounced the "puritanically moral language of orthodox Modern architecture" and favored a "messy vitality" described as hybrid, compromising, distorted, ambiguous, perverse, boring, conventional, accommodating, redundant, vestigial, inconsistent and equivocal.[2]

Critics of literature, art, and architecture were soon describing work that did not seem comfortably modern as postmodern. They saw postmodern literature as marked by a decline of the "metanarratives," the arching theories that centered upon European and North American conditions and explained them in humanistic, liberal terms. In art and architecture, postmodernism abandoned a style that valued the abstract, general statement over the detailed, the specific, the local. Modernism used, or professed to use, a single style that eliminated inconsistencies and, consequently, the record of the past; it claimed the professional whether artist, architect, or writer, as the sole creator of great art.[3]

Postmodernism became what modernism was not. It emphasized pluralism instead of unity, many stories rather than one, deconstruction of the metanarrative, the reintroduction of older styles and alternative styles, contradiction, ambiguity. Where modernism was clean and uncluttered, postmodernism might be double-coded—juxtaposing modernism and another style. In architecture this meant local, traditional styles could coexist with national styles. Although in practice postmodernism still sanctioned modern themes and a professionalized elite, in theory it allowed public participation in the creation of styles. It even allowed rural worlds to coexist with transcendent urban worlds. Most of us who came of age in the period since 1945 recognize these changes as a part of our own personal and professional lives. We are, in a sense, the first postmodern generation, although we carry much of the cultural baggage of modernism with us, learned from those who practiced it exceptionally well, defended it particularly fiercely, and double-coded for us so we accepted it as part of our postmodern world.[4]

In the first chapter I look at ideology through the stories women tell about creativity. I re-vision five creation stories that women have told about themselves in different arts and cultures. The Basketmaker, the Dancer, the Choreopoet, the Storyteller, and the Muralista are stories that may spur us on to look for more. I know much is yet to be found and unfolded.

In the second chapter I turn to biography, looking at the lives of three artists from what I call the Postfrontier Era, 1890 to 1920. I use biography as a way to explore how three individual women actually produced cultural artifacts—in this case baskets, paintings, and photographs. Each of these California women achieved enough success to have a significant amount of information about their lives collected by others. Joseppa Dick was among the best-known California basketmakers at a time when their art attracted international attention. Her baskets were sought after by anthropologists and by museum curators for their collections. Grace Hudson has an entire museum, next to her house in Ukiah, California, dedicated to preserving and interpreting her work. Emma Freeman's photographs are in the Newberry Library in Chicago and the California State Library in Sacramento. Each of these women lived at the borders where cultures met. Each over the course of her life created arts that reflected her own culture but in important ways also reflected a period in which cultures met in new uncharted ways.

I shift my focus from women artists as producers to their experiences with the marketplace in the third chapter. Between 1920 and 1945 some women found an important place in the markets of the art world. Here I look more carefully at the market for Indian baskets. I also examine the ways in which three Anglo-American women—Mary Austin, Georgia O'Keeffe, and Zoë Akins—interacted with markets for art. Modernism became the dominating cultural paradigm within which women and other artists had to sell their work. Mainstream America did not really accept modernism until the 1920s and 1930s and then only haltingly and partially.

In the fourth chapter, I try to come to terms with postmodernism, the period following World War II when the cultural center of modernism seemed to disintegrate. Lamenting that disintegration in California, author Joan Didion wrote: *the center does not hold*. I see this rather as an era of great possibilities where we should look even more intently at the borders rather than at the center. I have chosen to view these changes from the standpoint of audiences—who they were, and how they took form. I look specifically at the audiences for Pomo baskets, for western dances, and for the feminist art movement in southern California.

I have added two post-lecture chapters to this book. The fifth chapter takes western author Tillie Olsen's book *Silences* as a departing point. I look at the ways in which women have found their voices in the West and why. To analyze under what circumstances women began to write, I identified three literary traditions—anthropological, pioneer, and avant-garde. The anthropological tradition includes writing about indigenous peoples by Indian women and by middle-class Anglo women. The pioneer includes accounts by women of all ethnic settler groups. I discuss Anne Ellis as an example of the pioneer group. She wrote in detail about the process of beginning to write, a process we are just beginning to learn about for women of other ethnic groups. For the avant-garde tradition, I use Agnes Smedley, like Anne Ellis a working-class woman who could tell her story in print only because of the assistance of a small audience of middle-class supporters. This is merely an entry point, an attempt to listen to a few of the many voices that have overcome the silence that seems to surround so many women. The silences are many, but so also are the voices that we need to learn to hear.

In the final chapter I look at how theory may help us fix in memory the creative work of western women. This effort inevitably leads to work with postmodern theory. My own encounter with cultural history in the United States might help explain the context of postmodern theory and its relation to cultural history in the West.

In the early twentieth century, study of the United States was dominated by political and, to a lesser extent, economic history. What was left, historians often called intellectual history. It included literature, philosophy, theology, social theories, and sometimes music and art. In other words, the creations of brain workers, whatever medium they might choose to work in. In the 1960s, when I was a graduate student, we often read Perry Miller as the exemplar of intellectual history. As engaging and readable as his history was, in the 1960s it was far removed from the social changes we were experiencing, and there seemed no way to move it closer. As students we read contemporary philosophers and psychologists, such as Herbert Marcuse and Norman O. Brown, the sociologist C. Wright Mills, and many of the postwar poets and novelists who were just beginning to be labeled "the beats." In southern California, at least at the University of California, graduate students were reading such things. The melding of neo-Marxism, neo-Freudianism, and a type of American literary existentialism led many of us to social history as a retreat from a mainstream history devoted primarily to politics. A study of the social origins of political activities and policies offered the possibility of a deeper understanding of history.

The great flourishing of social history in the next thirty years led to rewriting American history, making room for women and African Americans, and in time for American Indians, Asian Americans, and Mexican Americans. Social historians had a practical bent. They wanted to know more about working people and how they had contributed to and benefited or suffered from the American political economy. Historians learned a great deal about social groups, whether ethnic, or gender-based, mostly middle or working class. Mainly, these groups built or serviced the society in some way. When historians used the term "cultures," it was in the way anthropologists used the term. It referred to the life ways of a people. Those who specifically wanted to study America came together to explore the varieties of that culture. The history of cultural workers, their lives and products, did not figure prominently in this historic universe except as examples of other parts of history. The only exception was the continued, if declining, interest in historians and historiography. Most social historians left the history of literature, art, and other traditional intellectual pursuits to their respective disciplines. It was a political generation that wanted to know more about social groups other than their own, meaning other than those that created the intellectual and artistic life of American culture and that did not seem to be agents of social change.

Historians, including historians of women, began to rediscover intellectual history in the 1980s. Under pressure from other disciplines, historians now looked at what had been intellectual history as a part of social or cultural history. They began to ask how people had created this part of culture, how intellectuals and artists functioned in society, and how they participated in the creation of belief structures. When historians returned to the study of this part of history, they found that it had become the province of theories developed primarily from other disciplines, in literature, psychology, and philosophy, a cluster of attitudes, assumptions, and questions loosely defined as postmodernism. In this last chapter, I try to explain how these theories may affect our writing of women's cultural history in the modern American West. I found this chapter on creating a memory the most challenging and difficult. I have tried to open a channel through which others may pass in creating a way to remember so that we may continue to use the cultural creativity of diverse women in our own contemporary work. I have consciously eliminated and excluded, as well as included. I hope the exclusions will invite others to challenge and critique, to fill in the wide open spaces that I have left.

I remember traveling across the wide open spaces as my parents took me from Minnesota to California, from east to west, across the plains and Rockies to the Pacific and then back again along old Route 66 when it was still a narrow, almost one-lane ribbon stretching across the West. I remember one stretch, I think it must have been through Tucumcari, New Mexico, that still had no white line. Even my father, usually slowed by neither roads nor climate, would not drive that section at night. From the time he managed to get his first car in the 1920s, he drove, I am told, like a demon. My first accident occurred when he wrecked a car while I was still in my mother's womb. It made her more timid than myself about high speed. Speed subdued her, and the constant moving from home to home, linked by what must have been terrifying drives along the ribbons of asphalt, turned her into a submissive woman. I remember, I must have been about fifteen, sitting next to my father in the front seat of our Chrysler as he gunned down a violent storm at ninety miles an hour, slowed only by the waves of water through which he plowed. My mother and grandmother sat thin-lipped and speechless in the back seat. I chose my words carefully. "I think you should slow down as this seems rather fast to be driving in the rain. And I think mother and grandmother are frightened." His foot immediately lifted off the accelerator. I had learned the power of carefully chosen words.

My life has followed the crescent of this story, up and down the roads of California, across Arizona, to New Mexico. It is the region I know best and the one that has seemed easiest for me to write about now. I have not required that the women whom I write about be born in this region; many of us were not. If they grew up here or had significant experiences here, experiences that became a part of their creativity, that was enough.

Part One

I

OUT THERE, OUT WEST
CREATION STORIES

Imagine for the moment that I am a storyteller who brings you stories about women from our collective western past. The tales I will tell are from five western American cultures. They are creation stories about the ways in which women become artists. In this chapter I briefly retell these stories and put them in context, then address how we as an audience can begin to read and understand them.

The stories come from women of five American cultural traditions— Indian, European, African, Asian, and Mexican. Each tells us something about western women and the creative process. I think of them not as disconnected pieces of a puzzle, but as transparencies lying one on top of the other, layers of our common culture through which we can see shapes and pattern and that we must understand separately and together.

I call these "creation stories of western women" because each presents a mythic vision of what it means to be a woman artist. Two of these stories are from the oral tradition. Three are texts by well-known women artists who grew up in the West and participated in western culture. I offer them as a way to begin looking at the creativity of western American women.

The Basketmaker

The first story, of Quail Woman, comes from northern California, from among the Pomoan speaking people. The people called Pomo by later settlers consider their homeland to be Clear Lake. Archaeologists say that about 2,500 years ago these people dispersed,

forming seven groups that each eventually spoke a distinct language. The people spread through what are today Lake,
Mendocino, and Sonoma counties and still reside there today. The
archaeology of basketry indicates a resemblance between the work
of these early California women and their eastern neighbors in
what is now Nevada. The basketry of the Pomo women became
the best known of all produced in California and has been in
great demand by Euro-American collectors and museums since
the late nineteenth century. Today, Pomo women still create baskets of great beauty.[1]

Pomo women's basketry is valued by Euro-Americans because
of the great variety of basket weaves and the dynamic outlook toward the designs in their baskets. The Pomo women developed elegant coiled baskets adorned with feathers and beads, which they
made in both single- and three-rod techniques. They also made
twined ware in seven techniques, including plain, diagonal, lattice,
and wrapped. Forms varied from very flat plate styles to almost perfect spheres. Canoe-shaped baskets of varying sizes were a Pomo
specialty. Designs were complex and also included a break, or
dau, in the design to show discontinuity. Textile archaeologist
Gene Weltfish wrote that when planning baskets, Pomo women
could choose from five different weaves; they could consider
weave as an element of design and shift weaves within the design. Weltfish, who studied the Pomo designs carefully, concluded
that the baskets embodied the women's striving for perfection
and that the designs were "an exquisite example of technical vir-
tuosity and creative art."[2]

Although early twentieth-century ethnologists asked Pomo women
about their designs, they seldom asked basketmakers to explain or interpret their own creativity. Collectors of baskets were much more interested in what the women had to say, and several left accounts that
indicate a rich oral tradition about the origin of basketmaking and the
dau. The records of Grace and John Hudson, who began collecting
baskets among the California Pomo in the late nineteenth century,
left one especially elaborate account. Grace and her husband, John,
collaborated on gathering Pomo oral traditions. The Hudsons wrote:
"The old folks tell the legend over and over to the young, urging
them not to forget or neglect the principles of the beautiful Quail

woman and their ancestors." The Hudsons published only brief versions of the Quail Woman story, but a longer unpublished version exists in their papers. This text is handwritten and dated 1903, a year during which John was making extensive field notes. The following story is based on his notes.[3]

Quail woman, Tcikaka, wants to learn basketry, so she goes to the lake shore and asks Bagil, the female water spirit, to instruct her. Bagil teaches her how to weave and to make the symbols. The two women work together for many years. Finally Bagil says, "You go home to your husband. He will not like this basketry, so you must hide it, but remember that I will watch and help you. Do not close up the symbols of my people but leave a path, a dau, open for me to go along with you from bottom to top of your work so I can inspect it." Bagil dives back into the lake and Tcikaka goes home with her work and secretly pursues basketry.

Her husband, the chicken hawk Tata, becomes violently jealous of her seclusion and beats her so that she leaves one night with her children and baskets. She ascends to the summit and hides in a lava cave. Tata searches everywhere for her, but the cave closes up whenever he approaches it, for Bagil looks after Tcikaka and sends her weaving materials to use. Tcikaka begins to change her shape. Her body grows strong and stands erect and her feet grow more like the human foot and the same with her children. One day she tries to escape, but every way she walks her tracks show like a quail so she takes a great basket and launches it and with her family floats down to the open water during the night. Her sisters, the quail plumes, hold up the basket so it will not sink, and she paddles south. During her voyages she is many times stopped by monsters who examine her basket and demand where she got it. Finally, they let her pass and she lands. Quail woman and her children become the first people.

The Dancer

The next story was told by the Euro-American woman Isadora Duncan, who revolutionized the art of dancing in the early twentieth century. Duncan grew up in California but left the United States to perform in Europe. She wrote her story between 1924 and her death in 1927. Boni and Liveright published it in 1927 as *My Life*. The original frontispiece bore a quote from Nietzsche's *Thus Spake Zarathustra*: "Everything heavy shall become light, every body a dancer and every spirit a bird."[4]

Duncan's story is of a woman's quest for freedom to develop and pursue her life's work. The book went through seven printings between December 1927 and May 1928 and sold millions of copies. It became a great myth of its time, wild, orgiastic, the conflict of art and love lived through the body of the great dancer as envisioned by herself.

Isadora begins her memoirs: "If people ask me when I began to dance I reply, 'In my mother's womb.'" She then traces her years in San Francisco as she learns to dance to the rhythm of the waves. "My life and my art were born of the sea.... I was already a dancer and a revolutionist." Duncan can wander by the sea because she has a poor working mother who does not confine her. "I was always in revolt against [school]," says Duncan. An infinite number of household moves take place, for her mother cannot pay the family bills. When she is only six Duncan begins a school for neighborhood tots. At ten she tells her mother it is a waste of time to go to school, that she will dance. The father is absent. Disgraced and divorced, he furnishes one grand house for a short time and makes two brief visits. The mother fills the home with music and poetry, the family begins to teach dance, and their fame spreads. An older woman friend incites Duncan to ambitious dreams by recounting the triumphs of a European ballerina, but Duncan rejects the ballet as too confining. She rejects marriage for the same reason. Instead she assumes responsibility for the family. The dominant note in the narrative is the constant spirit of revolt against what she sees as the narrowness and the limitations of her culture.

From Oakland, Isadora leads the "clan Duncan" eastward, first to Chicago, then to New York and London, finally to Paris, Berlin, Budapest, Florence, and on to Athens. This journey through the capitals of the Western world, accumulating Western culture, is accomplished in a spirit of innocence and joy. Isadora learns from great literature, especially Rousseau, Whitman, and Nietzsche, and from the museums in which the treasures of Western civilization are stored. The real American, she insists, is an idealist and a dreamer and she "a little, uneducated American girl, in some mysterious manner" finds the keys to unlock the hearts of the European intellectual and artistic elite.

During these years Duncan has many sexual adventures. She avoids being seduced by August Rodin, sending him away "bewildered," although she later regrets not giving her virginity to this "great god Pan." She flees the Loie Fuller dance troupe, so strange because the girls are stroking and kissing Loie, and portrays homosexuality as menacing. She describes one woman as an apparition in a black tailor-made suit with her hands in her pockets, "like some scarab of ancient Egypt," and a red-haired girl called Nursey who attacks her at 4 A.M. Frightened by her surroundings, Duncan leaves for Budapest. After leaving this threatening female world, the chaste nymph becomes a wild and careless Bacchante. She finds her Romeo, an actor practicing his part, and one night in a fury he carries her to his room and she, frightened but pitying him, submits to the "sheer torture" of sexual initiation. His joy and elation repay her for her suffering. Later they escape to the country for their first full night together, where she awakes "to find my hair tangled in his black scented curls, and to feel his arms around me." She learns the desire and the "furious abandon of this final moment." Romeo speaks of marriage but finally suggests she continue her career and leave him to his.

Duncan then transforms the sorrow, pain, and disillusion of love into her art. At Florence she sits for a day before the painting *Primavera* by Botticelli, dedicating herself to "dance the picture" and give to others "such ecstasy." Following triumphs in Berlin, she makes the trip to Athens, where she plans to teach the Greeks to dance and sing. She tells the Greeks to celebrate their gods and give up their terrible costumes. Finally, she reaches the amphitheater of Dionysus where the Duncans dance.

Remaining celibate after her affair with Romeo, Isadora now falls in love with a man who refuses to relieve her passion. Her nerves arrive "at that climax of love which is generally limited to the instant" but hums on insistently. Apollo, Dionysus, Christ, Nietzsche, and Richard Wagner battle for her soul. Then comes her first visit to Russia, her political awakening at seeing the coffins of the workers slain in the 1905 uprising, the continued frustration of her sexual desires. When Konstantin Stanislavsky refuses her sexual advances, she laments the fact that being a woman she cannot seek out a place of "doubtful reputation" to satisfy her need for sexual gratification. Instead, after a night of twisting and turning, she takes the baths to retone her system.

Back in Berlin, the Duncans decide to open a school of dance, like their other undertakings impractical, untimely, and impulsive. Then comes a lover she remembers for his "white, lithe, gleaming body," emerging from the "chrysalis of clothes." This is a great love, one she cannot reconcile with her own career. The aristocratic women of Berlin criticize Duncan's actions and she retorts with a strong public lecture on the "dance as an art of liberation" and "the right of woman to love and bear children as she pleased." Duncan becomes an unwed mother. This is too much for Duncan's own mother who abandons her and returns to San Francisco.

More lovers follow after motherhood. One is for pure pleasure. Another is a millionaire who supports her school and fathers a second child, but leaves when he discovers she is "a red-hot revolutionary." Finally Duncan recognizes that her life has a spiritual line; sometimes art puts a tragic end to love and sometimes love destroys art. Art and love are in constant battle. She ponders whether a woman can ever really be an artist. She has premonitions of little coffins, black crosses, women in black. The inevitable occurs: the death of her two children, who accidentally drown. A third child conceived with a stranger she meets on the shores of Italy also dies. Eventually, Duncan dedicates her energies to adopted children and to schools to teach children to dance.

In 1917 Duncan returns to the United States. Strapped for funds, by then an almost habitual condition, she accepts a contract to dance in California, twenty-two years after departing on her great adventure. She meets her mother, now haggard and old. Here is tragedy after high hopes, the inevitable condition of life.

In the last part of the book, Duncan develops the idea of herself as a spiritual offspring of Walt Whitman, creating a dance sprung from America, from nature, the Sierra Nevada, the Pacific as it washes the California coast, the great spaces of the Rocky Mountains, the Yosemite Valley, and Niagara Falls. She sketches out her vision of America dancing. American dance will have a rhythm as great as the exhilaration, the swing or curves of the Rocky Mountains. It will come out of the pioneer spirit, the gestures of the "redskins," a bit of Yankee Doodle, and the Irish jig. This tradition will come from the solar plexus, the waist up, to join Europe and the pyramids of Egypt and the Parthenon of Greece. "I see America dancing, standing with one foot poised on the highest point of the Rockies, her two hands stretched out from the Atlantic to the Pacific."

The Choreopoet

Ntozake Shange was born Paulette Williams in St. Louis, Missouri, in 1948, into a middle-class home that was a gathering place for black musicians, dancers, writers, and educators. During the 1970s Williams exchanged her birth name for Ntozake Shange—a Zulu name meaning "she who comes with her own things" and "she who walks like a lion"— and wrote of those early days. Her father, Shange recalled, was a painter before he became a surgeon; he kept a photographic darkroom in their St. Louis home where "images leapt out of his hands at all hours of the day and night, whenever he opened that door." The imaginative visual sweeps of her father "were courted by my mother's consistent and reverent readings of Dunbar, Shakespeare, Cullen, and Hughes, whose images were tactile and three dimensional for me." She grew up surrounded with "images, abstractions that drew warmth from me or wrapped me in loveliness."[5]

Shange went to Barnard College in New York, then west to the University of California, Los Angeles. In the early 1970s she moved to northern California where she taught at Sonoma State College and found "inspiration and historical continuity" in the Women's Studies Program, which offered courses on women as artists, women as poets, Third World women writers. The program, she wrote, became "inextricably bound to the development of my sense of the world, myself, & women's language. Such joy & excitement I knew in Sonoma, then I would commute back the sixty miles to San Francisco to study dance.... Knowing a woman's mind & spirit had been allowed me, with dance I discovered my body more intimately than I had imagined possible [and] a clearer understanding of my voice as a woman & a poet." Women's Studies rooted her to an "articulated female heritage & imperative," and dance study with Raymond Sawyer and Ed Mock showed that "everything African and colloquial was hers." She danced with Halifu Osumari's black women's dance troupe, tracing "The Spirit of the Dance" from western Africa through the African Diaspora to popular jazz dance. After some seventy-three performances, she left to begin production of *for colored girls who have considered suicide/when the rainbow is enuf*.[6]

for colored girls drew on several sources. One was the dance and music Shange had been studying and the ideas being experimented with in the San Francisco dance community. The central concept was finding creativity in common people through dance. The community of women poets in the Bay Area was experimenting with similar ideas. Judy Grahn had just written "The Common Woman Poems." In the summer of 1974 Shange began a series of seven poems, modeled on

Grahn's, to explore the realities of seven different kinds of women, nameless women. From this idea she developed with others the choreopoetry that became *for colored girls*. It is entitled "for colored girls", Shange said later, because "that's who it was for. I wanted them to have information that I did not have. I wanted them to know what it was truthfully like to be a grown woman. I didn't know. All I had was a whole bunch of mythology—tales and outright lies."[7]

First performed in the Bay Area, *for colored girls* opened at the Bacchanal, a woman's bar outside Berkeley, in December 1974. It was performed at Sper's, an old beat hangout in San Francisco, then at the "new" Malvina's, the Coffee Gallery, the Rippletad, and finally at Minnie's Can-Do Club in Haight-Ashbury. In 1975 the troupe left to do the show at Studio Rivbea in New York. By December, when the play had been restaged for the New York audience, it contained some twenty poems. The words, said Shange, were of black girls growing up, their triumphs and errors, their struggle to become "all that is forbidden by our environment, all that is forfeited by our gender, all that we have forgotten."[8]

for colored girls weaves together the stories of seven young African American women, each identified by color and city rather than name. The prologue, spoken by the lady in brown, speaks about the necessity to "sing a black girl's song... to know herself / to know you"

> sing her song of life
> she's been dead so long
> closed in silence so long
> she doesn't know the sound
> of her own voice[9]

The poems begin with the young women recounting their lives and loves. The lady in blue says "i love you more than poem." Gradually the lady in orange (played by Shange in the original performances) becomes the oracle:

> i'm a poet
> who writes in english
> come to share the worlds witchu

The lady in purple moves backward in time becoming Sechita, Egyptian goddess of creativity, goddess of love "performin the rites / the conjurin of men / conjurin the spirit."

The lady in red becomes the "passion flower of southwest los angeles" who sends her lover off at 4:30 A.M. because she had

> a lot of work to do/ & i cant
> with a man around/

When she finished writing "the account of her exploit in a diary"

> she placed a rose behind her ear
> & cried herself to sleep

The visions become darker. The lady in blue speaks of being cleansed by the waters of the Pacific. Now, in Harlem, her "ankles are coated in grey filth." The stories tell of rape, back room abortions, betrayals by other women, then their coming together. The lady in purple holds the head of a friend on her lap:

> the lap of her sisters soakin up tears
> each understandin how much love stood between them
> how much love between them
> love between them
> love like sisters[10]

Like an oracle the lady in orange returns:

> ever since i realized there waz someone callt
> a colored girl an evil woman a bitch or a nag
> i been tryin not to be that & leave bitterness
> in somebody else's cup/…
> …/especially cuz i can make
> the music loud enuf /so there is no me but dance /& when
> i can dance like that /there's nothing cd hurt me /…
> this is a requiem for myself /cuz i
> have died in a real way /…
> …cuz i had convinced
> myself colored girls had no right to sorrow/ & i lived
> & loved that way & kept sorrow on the curb /allegedly
> for you /but i know i did it for myself/
> i cdnt stand it
> i cdnt stand bein sorry & colored at the same time
> it's so redundant in the modern world[11]

The quest continues, with the lady in purple saying:

> lemme love you just like i am /a colored girl /i'm finally bein
> real /no longer symmetrical & impervious to pain

The lady in yellow speaks:

…my dance waz not enuf /& it waz all i had
but bein alive & bein a woman & bein colored is a metaphysical
dilemma /i havent conquered yet /do you see the point
my spirit is too ancient to understand the separation of
soul & gender /my love is too delicate to have thrown
back on my face[12]

The lady in green then gives a long complaint about somebody
who "almost walked off wid alla my stuff"

this is a woman's trip & i need my stuff /…
this is mine/ ntozake 'her own things'/ that's my name /…
…i want my own things /how i lived them/
& give me my memories /how i waz when i waz there/
you cant have them or do nothin wit them /[13]

Somebody almost got away with her

me in a plastic bag under their arm /me
danglin on a string of personal carelessness/[14]

The climax comes as the lady in red tells the story of "crystal and
beau willie brown," how the father of crystal's children, driven crazy by
his experiences in Vietnam, drops them from the fifth-floor apartment.

Finally, there is the laying on of hands, all the gods coming into the
women, "the holiness of myself released." And the final benediction:

i found god in myself
& i loved her /i loved her fiercely

The lady in brown, who opened the service, has the final words:

& this is for colored girls who have considered
suicide /but are movin to the ends of their own
rainbows

A creative life is now possible because the women have found affir-
mation within.

The Storyteller

Maxine Hong Kingston was living in Hawaii when she wrote *The
Woman Warrior* in the early 1970s. Knopf published the book in 1976;
it won the National Book Critics Circle award that year and has sold

well ever since in hardback and soft cover. In 1976 the University of Hawaii hired Kingston as a professor and in 1980 Hawaii made her a National Treasure. Kingston was born in 1940 in the central California town of Stockton where her parents ran a laundry. She went to public schools, attended the University of California at Berkeley from 1958 to 1962, and taught English for fifteen years in Hayward, California, and later in Hawaii.

The Woman Warrior is a memoir of the creation of a female story-teller. The book begins with the mother telling stories to the daughter and ends with the mother and daughter collaborating in a story, the first part told by the mother, the last part by the daughter who has now become a part of the storytelling tradition. The book, as Kingston said in another context, was the story of consciousness emerging and a human being deciding how to create his or her own life. Kingston refers to the narrator in *The Woman Warrior* as "that narrator girl...so coherent and intense always, throughout...an intensity of emotion that makes the book come together."[15]

People who tell stories, Kingston writes, "don't always flatter themselves in their stories," but "come from a tradition of story telling, and so they know about form. A lot of times they like to play around," and to twist things around. "That's why I made myself such a strong character, because knowing this narrator and her biases and her propensity for colorfulness, you'd say aha *she would* think that story's true."[16]

The narrator girl tells us how she becomes a storyteller but she does not make it easy to know. Don't forget, says Kingston, that Chinese myths do not help Chinese Americans in their life. They need to be changed and integrated into their lives; it is an ongoing problem for people who have a different home culture from the public culture. Instead of being shocked into silence, Kingston uses the Chinese tradition to speak, for within the Chinese tradition the myths change from one telling to another.

The girl narrator, the one who can talk story, must go through a special training by her mother. Her mother tells stories—such as "The Warrior Woman"—that have become cultural myths. Stories so old, repeated so often, that they have achieved a wide telling and a wide listening. There are family stories, passed on through the oral tradition and not to be told outside the family, and village stories that are to be repeated only to certain groups. The narrator girl serves her apprenticeship as learner. But she must also be able to translate the stories to a written form, be able to tell stories that translate well into another language, for she is becoming a storyteller for another culture. Her final story is a retelling of the story of the poet Ts' ai Yen, who is captured by the barbarians at age twenty. Her children do not speak Chinese, yet she finds a voice that can be understood by her captors who do not speak her language and by her children who learn to sing along. The songs, later brought back to the home culture, translate well. Thus, the poet, singer, storyteller communicates to both cultures.

The five stories told by the narrator girl are complexly interwoven. The first is about No-name Woman who becomes pregnant while her husband is in America. The villagers attack her home because they fear her pregnancy will bring bad luck, and No-name woman, after birthing her child, drowns herself in the village well. The second story is of Fa Mu Lan, the woman warrior. In the third, Brave Orchid tells her own story as warrior woman; in the fourth, set in America, she fails to save her sister. The fifth story is the storyteller creating an identity, self-creation. I will tell only the fifth, the last story.

This is the narrator girl's own story: how she learns to talk-story and become a storyteller who can design and tell her own stories. Her most difficult task is learning to speak English because she is taught only Chinese by her parents. "When I went to kindergarten and had to speak English for the first time, I became silent," she says. During the first silent year, black students talk to and protect her, but she speaks to no one and flunks kindergarten. Later she finds out she cannot be silent but must become an American "I," which is not as complex as the Chinese "I." She paints black pictures for three years, scores zero on her IQ tests, but finally begins to learn to speak English.

Meanwhile, she attends Chinese language school each afternoon and becomes fluent in Chinese. This knowledge is taught not for her own use, but so she can speak about the Chinese culture and for the Chinese. She is warned especially not to report what she calls the deformities, or crimes, of the culture. By the sixth grade, the narrator girl is "arrogant with talk," but when she tries to get another silent Chinese girl to talk, she fails.

The result of this failure is a mysterious eighteen-month illness that forces her to miss the last part of grammar school and her first year in junior high school. The silent narrator girl, who is taken care of and sheltered by her family, speaks only Chinese during her illness. She forgets English. To become a talk-story person she must learn to talk in English. Not to talk would bring insanity. The narrator girl says: "Insane people were the ones who couldn't explain themselves. There were many crazy girls and women ... there were adventurous people inside my head to whom I talked." She wonders if her sister has similar mind people and asks casually, "do you talk to people that aren't real inside your mind." "Do I *what*," the sister demands, and the narrator girl quickly says, "Never mind. Nothing."

Then comes a period when relatives and villagers believe she should be married. At first she tries to make herself "unsellable" in America, banking on their plans to send to China for a husband after it is liberated from the Communists. When the Communist Party manages to maintain control, these plans are replaced with schemes to marry off daughters in America. She begins to notice the role of the daughter-in-law in Chinese Opera from Hong Kong where the new daughter-in-law sings, "beat me, beat me" and the audience—men and women— laugh. Her father tells her about the right of Confucian males to kill disobedient wives and how women sing old songs about being faithful to husbands.

The girl narrator increases her attempts to be unattractive. As eligible males disappear and a mentally handicapped boy appears, she throws off her assumed defects, studies hard, and gets A's in school. Meanwhile, she says, "[I] had grown inside me a list of over two hundred things that I had to tell my mother so that she would know the true things about me and stop the pain in my throat." Like other creative women when they are unable to create, she is unable to speak and the unspoken causes serious psychosomatic illness. "My throat hurt constantly, vocal cords taut to snapping." Finally her fear that the family will marry her off to the retarded boy unleashes her voice. She shouts: "I am not going to be a slave or a wife....I won't let you turn me into a slave or a wife. I'm getting out of here....I'm never getting married, never."

The daughter accuses her mother of cutting her tongue to make her stop talking. Her mother retorts that she cut it to make her talk more, not less, that she did not plan to marry her off, that she "can't even tell a joke from real life .... Can't even tell real from false ... who'd want to marry you anyway.... I don't see why you can't be a doctor like me .... I don't see why you need to go to college at all to become either one of those things....Why don't you go to typing school? I fixed your tongue so you could say charming things." Girl narrator retorts: "When

I get to college, it won't matter if I'm not charming. And it doesn't matter if a person is ugly; she can still do schoolwork." The mother says she didn't say she was ugly: "That's what we're supposed to say. That's what Chinese say. We like to say the opposite."

In the telling, the girl narrator's list of grievances grows. She has at last created herself as storyteller but is now an outlaw knot-maker to her mother. Her mother tells her to get out, shouting "Ho Chi Kuei."

Kingston leaves very few pages to resolve this expulsion by the mother, though we know from earlier pages the daughter will return, be called affectionately "Little Dog" by her mother. In the last few pages of the book the narrator girl deals with the separation by saying, "I had to leave home in order to see the world logically, logic the new way of seeing." She looks up the meaning of "Ho Chi Kuei" in books and finds complex meanings. Kuei clearly means ghost but Ho Chi can mean anything from water lily to grub. Maybe she says, it has a simpler explanation and it means ghosts who have advantages, or have it so easy. The throat pain, she says, always returns, "unless I tell what I really think....I continue to sort out what's just my childhood, just my imagination, just my family, just the village, just names, just living."

In the last pages, the girl narrator tells her mother, "I also talk story." Then she tells a story about her grandmother, proving "one family was immune to harm as long as they went to plays." The girl narrator then says she hopes that at some of these performances they heard the songs of Ts' ai Yen. And she tells her story last: the woman storyteller brings about inter-ethnic harmony through integration of the arts. She plays the flute, and the barbarians can hear her, her children can hum along, and she can take her art back to her own people.

Muralista

Judy Baca is a *muralista*, a public artist, who chose to tell her story orally. In three major interviews during the 1980s and in the catalog of the exhibit *Body/Culture: Chicano Figuration*, published by Sonoma State University in 1990, she provided her personal and political story as a woman artist.[17]

Baca tells two types of stories. Some lead outward to her place as a public artist. Others move inward to her cultural traditions as a mestiza—a woman of mixed race—and a healer. Together they become a complex story of her life as an artist.

The stories begin with her grandmother in Mexico during the Revolution of 1912. They move through her mother's youth in Colorado, to Watts in southern California, then her own youth in the San Fernando Valley, her work in East Los Angeles, and then to Venice, southwest of Los Angeles. Through these stories Baca finds a way to join her grandmother's concept of domestic art and of community healing to a sense of herself as Chicana, mestiza, artist, feminist.

Baca's grandmother is a central and stable figure in both these journeys. She hides money in a pitcher, which allows the family to escape after banditos destroy their small business in Mexico. She raises her family in La Junta—a town of Mexican railroad workers and migrant workers segregated from an Anglo minority—and tries to keep the family there, then follows her daughter to California, taking along two sisters to form a female family.[18]

The grandmother is a crucial influence. "My grandmother," Judy remembered, "did very delicate crocheting, in which she would make these amazing doilies, like three-dimensional doilies that would stand up on the tables, and they were carefully ironed, of different flower arrangements...she didn't have patterns for them...they were just made.... And we had altars in our home, in which there were candles and flower arrangements and the pictures of the santos, and...they were sort of...precious areas that were set aside and made beautiful." Her grandmother, Judy said, was "very spiritual, very Indian-looking... a tremendous spiritual force...she prayed and made things that would heal you...the absolute foundation of my confidence. I know my sense of self was formed at that time." Later, when Judy graduated from college, it was her grandmother who asked her, "What's it for?" Judy then decided to use her skill to speak to the people she most cared about, family and community.[19]

Judy's mother provided a second tradition. Her story was one of rebellion. She hated La Junta and at eighteen, when her father died, left for California. By the end of World War II she was in Watts, where her daughter Judy was born in 1947. The father was in the military, left for the Pacific before Judy was born, and was reported missing in action. Judy's mother raised her in a female household, speaking no English. When Judy started school and the teachers would not let Judy speak Spanish, the mother taught her daughter flawless English. Education, she told Judy, was a way to avoid suffering. Early in 1953 she married an Anglo, taking her daughter to a lower-middle-class neighborhood in the San Fernando Valley, then pushing her to attend the all-Anglo State University at Northridge. "I was the first Baca to go to college," Judy remembered, "a journey out of my neighborhood . . . slowly the world opened to me, a big metal door that had been clamped shut for centuries. It was like a tiny, tiny creaking, creaking and creaking until I saw little bits of light—and possibilities."[20]

Thus Judy inherited both worlds, that of her Mexican grandmother who remembered the old traditions and that of her Mexican American mother who saw new skills as a way to escape to a new, freer world. Judy drew in kindergarten while she learned English, drew in grammar school while she learned the culture of San Fernando Valley, and in Catholic high school where she practiced her first public art, drawing naked nuns running across the blackboard with their habits flying. "I was punished regularly for that," she said. In 1969 she graduated from college with a major in art and a minor in history and education. She still wanted to paint.[21]

But how could she combine her cultural traditions with the public traditions available for her? An art based on western European models that could be put into galleries would silence her own traditions. "Images I grew up with in my home had no representation in that world," she said. "There was no aesthetic I knew—a certain exuberance for color, for example—that was validated in the art world. I thought to myself, if I get my work into galleries, who will go there? People in my family had never been to a gallery in their entire lives. My neighbors never went to galleries. All the people I knew didn't go to galleries. . . . I had no way to apply my work to that structure. You couldn't take an aesthetic that wasn't mainstream into the galleries and have it accepted—especially as a woman, and especially as a Chicana."[22]

Instead Judy chose to work within the Chicano Art Movement. There she joined artists—mostly men—in a search for self-definition. "What part of me was Indian, and what part was Spanish? Was the mestizo a blending of the two, or did I actually embody, as I feared, the historic struggle between these cultures while displaced in the third culture of an Anglo-dominated country?" She did not know the answers but she ended up in an East Los Angeles barrio working with kids in gangs, the "throwaway people" she called them. No one wanted them in the parks and no one wanted them leaving their marks on the walls, the marks that told "who they were, who they hung out with, what generation they were, how many of them had the same nickname—all in what they call *placayasos*....It has to do with people saying, 'Listen, I am nothing here. So I am your wall. Here's who I am.'" There at the bottom, with these youth no one wanted, these youth everyone hoped would just disappear, who created by leaving their marks on walls, Judy found a way to use symbols made by the community to create new symbols acknowledging people's commonality. She began to work with the young people to create giant murals that would tell their stories.[23]

From 1970 to 1974 the East Los Angeles murals multiplied until you could drive through and see the powerful pieces everywhere. Judy was able to obtain a grant from the city of Los Angeles to expand the program to other ethnic communities. The murals contrasted the dream of America with the reality that these youths faced—police brutality, exploitation of undocumented workers, the viciousness of urban renewal. More than one thousand people worked on 250 murals. In 1977 Judy began a monumental project called *The Great Wall*, which snakes through the San Fernando Valley on the concrete sides of the drainage canals.

In the course of becoming a public artist, Judy also struggled to define her role as a woman artist. There were no role models, she said, "to be a woman essentially alone and willing...to put my work first in my life and deal with what that might mean." What it meant for Judy was that in the course of the mural projects she "stopped being married" and moved to Venice and smack dab into the feminism of the Venice women's community. She met other professional women who took her art seriously. But, Judy recalled, "I always felt like I was a visitor in a certain way, because there were not that many Latin women, or Third World women, at all." A "visitor" with the women's group and an "oddity" in the Chicano culture was how she described herself. Nevertheless, she made good friends. With some of them she founded the nonprofit Social and Public Art Resource Center (SPARC), to document the murals with slides. She also met Judy Chicago who was working on the mammoth Dinner Party project, depicting historical women as creative women, and the middle-class women who had volunteered to create that project. Those women wanted self-esteem, Baca thought. The people who had worked with her needed money to live on.[24]

Through the women's art movement, Baca came to see her mural work in a new way. "I think all this work I have been doing is about healing, and it's about developing some kind of loving approach to the world, in which I can use my skills....I make images—to heal a social environment and a physical environment." The healing, she thought, came from her grandmother. Her grandmother's prayer and healing translated through art into a way to overcome powerlessness as woman and as Chicana; a way to fuse the multiple cultural heritages of the West.[25]

That is the last of the five stories: Quail Woman, the Basketmaker; Duncan, the Dancer; Kingston, the Storyteller; Shange, the Choreopoet; and Baca, the Muralist. All are different in form. The cultures are different, the lives are different. Each richly evokes the image of women as creative artists in the West. But how should we read these stories? Are there alternative readings?

I think these stories tell us something about becoming conscious of humanity and gender through cultural work, about how to understand this work, and how to remember it. Each of these stories asks us to understand the experience of the women who have tried to create in their cultures—as basketmaker, dancer, storyteller, choreopoet, muralist. Each has as a central theme, the experience of women. But each has a different path; each is embedded within a different culture.

In her recent book *Grandmothers of the Light*, Paula Gunn Allen describes stories such as Quail Woman as ritual guides, examples of spirituality that have a healing power available to all. Quail Woman is a story about women teaching women, about the quest for a focus of creative energies and how that work can be transforming and healing.[26] Quail Woman must resist her husband who does not wish her to create, to become human; and she must escape the monsters that wish to stop her on her voyage toward humanness. She has assistance from female spirits in nature—the water spirit who teaches and protects her and the quail plumes who help her on her voyage. Each time a woman weaves a basket, she reminds herself of how the first woman learned to weave and how the first teacher will return to inspect her work. The dau is a break that interrupts her pattern, a discontinuity that allows space for inspection of her work. Together the story of Quail Woman and the baskets that the women create remind the entire community of their origins and their quest to become a people.

When we turn from this quest story to the stories of women in other cultures, the contrast is quite evident. Duncan also describes her quest as an attempt to reconcile art and life. While individual males may inhibit that quest, the male intellectual traditions also nurture her quest. The male traditions do not, however, recognize female genius in art, or women's sexuality. Women are supposed to choose heterosexual love, to contain their sexuality, and to abandon art. Duncan safely achieves heterosexual love and children during her quest, but she refuses to give up art. Her punishment is losing her children. For Duncan, the monsters are within as well as outside, and she must fight them alone.

Shange's colored girls also undertake a quest for their creativity. But Shange warns that their quest must end almost entirely within. The external monsters take the form of women as well as men. Only women's songs, their stories, can help them find their way through the terrors that may be inflicted on them because of their color and their sex, and which may lead them to self-destruction through suicide. Their journey toward creativity is to find the creative core within. Each woman has a creative life within her that must withstand and grow with the hard experiences she will endure. The collective help of women is needed as well. Not an orange or a purple woman, but a rainbow of women is "enough."

The quest by Kingston's storyteller and Baca's quest are more complicated, for these women must negotiate two cultures and two languages. It is here that we become most conscious of western women as living in the borderlands. These women are on two shores at once; they cross cultures and move along the borders between cultures in ways that we must learn if we wish to create a truly multicultural history.

For our quest as narrators of western women's cultural history we have the assistance of other women writers. Like the dau, their comments can interrupt our patterns and leave space for the inspection of our work. Gayatri Spivak, bell hooks, and Gloria Anzaldúa all provide insights about how we can move toward a multicultural history. I will return to these authors in a later chapter; I wish to briefly note here how their writings can force us to interrupt past patterns to allow the stories of many women to be told.

From Gayatri Spivak we can learn to be aware of our position as the central narrator in our cultural stories. These cultural stories, she argues, carry messages about subordination and counterinsurgency that we can decipher if we become conscious of ourselves as central narrators and the dominant, conservative nature of that position. Spivak is most concerned here with the domination of Western European and American attitudes that are transmitted along with cultural stories. By looking critically at a story and by analyzing its parts—deconstructing is one of the words sometimes applied to this process—we can see how a cultural story displaces other stories and subordinates them to a lower status. In a sense, as storytellers in our own right, we do this to the stories we tell that become subordinate in our telling. Spivak's message puts us in a hall of mirrors where we are made aware of the role we play as narrators who interact with the subjects of our stories in complex ways that must be constantly reexamined. When I tell the story of Quail Woman, for example, I will not be able to disentangle myself from the story in telling it. I am appropriating it and I must be conscious of that process. In what Spivak calls a postcolonial world, one cannot ignore gender or culture as a source, or potential source, of domination.[27]

Or race, bell hooks would argue insistently. For hooks the task is to move out of philosophical structures rooted in racial bias. Because American culture has been rooted so deeply in the socially constructed theories and practice of race, this task is not a simple one. The image of America as a dancer that Duncan chooses as her cultural icon is lodged in a bicultural concept that merges various European-based dance traditions to Native American ones but totally rejects the African American dance heritage. The Rockies then become not just a pleasant home location for this dancing America, but one chosen to exclude as well as include. Duncan is trying desperately to become a creator of American myths as well as her own. America dances in her image and allows her a place in its creative past. She does not allow African Americans into this chosen location. Only by looking at Shange's vision of the power of black dance and culture in contrast to Duncan's vision can we really see how race and culture can create cultural divides.[28]

Gloria Anzaldúa reminds us that in the Southwest cultures have mixed in ways that can either exclude or include. From her, we can learn to see Maxine Hong Kingston and Judy Baca as prototypes of Pacific Southwestern women who must negotiate a number of cultures, crossing from one to the other over cultural divides.[29]

These then are the divides, the frontiers, over which we must travel if we wish to begin to understand the lives of women who helped create America's cultures. Can we "out here, out West" begin to create a ground that belongs to no one, that really explains the creativity of women in different cultures? Can we tell the stories of western women and our own stories powerfully enough so that they become the collective stories of western peoples, men and women?

I think we can create a history of women and creativity in the modern American West. We can begin to know how women have transferred their energy to visual, performing, and literary arts, how those arts have been distributed and transmitted, and how audiences have received them in the past. We can ask why other women artists are silent or silenced. And how to remember those who are not. In the next chapters, I explore these questions, looking at the lives of some creative western women, the contexts within which their work was bought and sold, and how they struggled to find audiences for their work.

2

AN ENERGY OF THEIR OWN
THE ARTISTS

The creation stories of western women that I told in the first chapter—of Quail Woman, Isadora Duncan, Ntozake Shange, Maxine Hong Kingston, and Judy Baca—were inspirational visions of the struggles by western women to become creative artists. They were stories told from within the process. Another way to look at the lives of creative women is from the outside, as lives embedded in specific historical cultures and contexts. Creation stories enlighten because they transmit information about the creative process. The stories of the lives and works of artists convey a different kind of enlightenment, which comes from understanding the interaction between the artist and her times.

I am not quite sure how to describe the purpose of an artist. I suppose it is to transmit her personal energy to an art form through the techniques and standards of her culture and to transform them. An artist, wrote Virginia Woolf, "in order to achieve the prodigious effort of freeing whole and entire the work that is in [her], must be incandescent." I like the word incandescent—strikingly bright, radiant, or clear; marked by brilliance, glowing.[1]

Woolf was writing of the crippling effect that hostility and indifference to their work had on women artists within European culture. Where European-based cultures dominated women artists from different cultural traditions, they had the additional burden of colonialism. To be incandescent these women had to maintain their vitality in the face of the uneven and sometimes hidden injuries within the web of gender and colony. In order to create, women artists had to sharpen their skills and preserve their energy against great odds.

To explore how women created their art I focus on the period from 1890 to 1920 and on a trio of artists in northern California—Joseppa Dick, Grace Hudson, and Emma Freeman. These artists were all involved in the coming together of cultures that marked this period. All were well known and financially successful. They all left important bodies of work. Dick, a Central Pomo, created baskets of great beauty. Grace Hudson painted portraits of the Pomo, sometimes with great power. Emma Freeman's best photographs of older Native American people convey the quiet dignity with which they survived the harsh coming together of Indian and Euro-American cultures in northern California.

I have chosen northern California as a focus for this look at artists in the period from 1890 to 1920 because it was an area in which many women produced art. Collecting of American Indian baskets by Anglo-Americans encouraged the weaving of thousands of art baskets by Indian women in California. At the same time, the changing attitudes toward women as artists in the Anglo-American culture brought hundreds of them into the art market, many after formal training in skills such as painting, which males had formerly reserved primarily for themselves. Photography, in which new techniques made creative experiment more important than formal training, also offered new opportunities for women. A demand developed for photographs of local landscapes, and portraits. Women eagerly exploited this market. The changes in the art market allowed space to redefine what was art, who could be an artist, and how art should be valued.

Much of this experimentation went on in the urban San Francisco Bay area of California, but Dick, Hudson, and Freeman produced their art in rural areas. Small towns provided places where women who had contacts with urban markets could create without some of the constraints of an urban life-style. In the late nineteenth century, urban dwellers placed a premium on the rural life that these women lived. Many city folk considered these rural areas remnants of the past, which they nostalgically wished to capture through accumulating collections of art work. In northern California American Indians were experiencing the cultural domination of Anglo-American immigrants even more than previously, but many maintained their determination to create separate cultures that would retain their most important traditions. At the borders of these cultures were women and men who moved between both cultures. Dick, Hudson, and Freeman moved along these borders, conforming to some of their cultures' traditions, but also moving out of them as they created baskets, paintings, and photographs for the urban market.

Thousands of Indian women in the West were creating art without canvas or paper, with pottery, weaving, beading, and basketry. The Indian cultures of the West supported these artistic activities of women, not only because they retained and strengthened cultures but also because they provided sources of income for Indian women for whom the Anglo-American economy provided only poorly paying jobs, usually as household workers in areas distant from their homes. Art work allowed women to remain at home rather than migrating to find these poorly paying jobs. It also allowed them to maintain, adapt, and create culture in the face of the permanent presence and control by Anglo-Americans. As long as the women also educated children in these skills, and engendered a respect for them, the cultures could be passed on. The arts and crafts movement of the 1880s popularized Indian baskets in the East and helped create a demand for Joseppa's baskets.

Early in October 1901, Joseppa stood at the edge of the grave of her only son, Billy. Three years earlier, eleven-year-old Billy had left for a government boarding school in Oregon. The school had returned Billy to Joseppa, racked with tuberculosis, just a few days before his death. Joseppa was giving Billy a traditional Pomo burial by destroying her art and burying it with him. She cut into quarters a fine feathered basket on which she had worked for several years and threw that into the grave. Then she threw in all her other finished baskets, large and small, and all the baskets on which she was still working. She then stripped her house of all its contents—the sewing machine and cook stove, all the furniture and clothing—and burned them. A Euro-American law prohibited her from burning her house, but her father burned his barn, a good buggy, and harness. When Joseppa's husband, Jeff, became ill soon after the funeral, Joseppa sat by his side in the empty house working incessantly on a new basket. She planned to sell the basket for beads to bury with Jeff should he die.[2]

The image of Joseppa destroying her art at the grave of her son and creating it at the bedside of her sick husband contrasts greatly with the

following one of Grace Hudson. The year was 1898. Joseppa had come
from Yokayo, a Pomo community six miles south of Ukiah, to Grace
Hudson's studio to pose for her. After sketching Joseppa, Grace Hudson
completed an oil painting. She called it *Back to Her Tribe*. The painting depicted Joseppa as a single mother returning to her village, holding
her son, Billy, in her arms. Joseppa was barefoot. Her long hair was
pulled back. She wore a simple blouse and calf-length full skirt. After
completing the painting, Hudson carefully photographed the painting
and numbered it 123. Then she gave it to her husband, John, to market. Shortly after Billy's death and burial, John sold the painting for
five hundred dollars.[3]

Art had different meanings in the cultures of Joseppa and Grace
in this period. But in a way both were experimenting with their art.
Joseppa used her art for traditional ceremonial purposes, but she marketed and sold it as well. By practicing her art, she was able to strengthen
cultural traditions and to further its continuation. At the same time
her art allowed her to participate more fully in the settler culture and
the Anglo market. Grace sold her art in a market where few Anglo
women ventured. The practice of her art took her away from what was
a traditional Anglo woman's culture—creating within and for the
home—into a new space where she created for the public and mingled
with the public as an artist. She moved expertly within the market,
looking for traders who would recognize her own cultural artistic
standards and allow her to control form and design while still meeting
market demands.

Coming from a centuries old tradition of women's basket art, Joseppa
understandably chose that technique within which to express her creativity. Her people, the Central Pomo, had migrated west from Clear
Lake toward the coast years before and settled in the area later known
as Mendocino County. Among the Pomo, Quail Woman was honored
as the first basketmaker and the first human. Like other Pomo
basketmakers, Joseppa left a break, or dau, in each basket design so
that Quail Woman could enter to inspect the quality of the work and
see that it was properly constructed. Joseppa was well known among
traders for her fine work and recognized by thousands of people through
her demonstrations in California and New Mexico. Her baskets, which
now lie scattered in museums and private collections, were truly exceptional works of art, created through great effort as she struggled to

*Noted Pomo basketmaker Joseppa Dick with her son Billy Peters and husband
Jeff Dick at Yokayo Rancheria. Photograph by Henry W. Henshaw, 1892.
Courtesy Grace Hudson Museum.*

adapt to the new marketplace. For Joseppa and the other Pomo
basketmakers, art was more than something sold for money, as welcome as that may have been. The art of basketmaking gave vitality
to a culture under great pressure to deculture itself. Euro-Americans saw baskets as remnants of a dying culture. For Native American women, the baskets they created were symbols of a living culture still being handed down by women to their daughters and kin.[4]

By 1900 the Pomo had largely lost the need for functional baskets.
They now had access to metal pots and buckets, easily purchased with
money received for wage work. Baskets for daily use were rapidly declining, as were baskets for ceremonial use, in part because Pomos were
abandoning the ceremonies that used them. Joseppa's decision to follow the traditional burial ceremonies was a powerful way to reinforce

the older culture; baskets played a particularly important role in these ceremonies. Among the Pomo, baskets accompanied the dead as they were cremated. Wealth might be measured by the number and quality of baskets thus burned. As the Pomo adopted Christianity, missionaries and officials urged Pomo to bury their dead and abandon their traditional ceremonial customs. Collectors also urged Pomo to sell rather than destroy the baskets. One anthropologist was horrified that Joseppa wished to destroy her fine feathered basket at the burial of her son and tried to dissuade her. Her determination to do so was a particularly strong statement about the primacy of culture over market despite the increasing economic importance of the latter among Pomo women. The destruction of her own art was a symbol of Joseppa's identification with her people and their common history.[5]

The market baskets that Joseppa created were not traditional baskets. They were art baskets, objects that she exchanged for cash to pay for desirable manufactured items. Although women like Joseppa chose to continue some traditional forms, design elements, and colors, they usually reworked baskets in new ways for the market. Joseppa joined other California basketmakers during the height of the craze for California baskets in creating tiny miniatures that were popular with collectors in the East. One measured five thirty-seconds of an inch at its largest diameter.[6]

Joseppa was born around 1860 near Echo, in Sonoma County, California. Her parents may have been among the people forcibly brought from their inland home to Mendocino Indian Reserve established by the U.S. government in 1856. Nearly half the Pomo refused to go to the reservation; others continued to escape from it. Finally, in 1867 the government declared the reservation a failure and closed it. The Pomo made their way home to find that during their imprisonment Anglo settlers had occupied their lands. Some of their villages had been plowed under for agricultural fields. Wild game and food had almost disappeared because the Anglo settlers had introduced cultivation and cattle. With no land and no food, some Indians went to work as laborers on the farms and ranches of the Anglos.[7]

Among four groups of Pomo who refused this way of life were Joseppa's parents. In 1881 they joined with other Pomos to purchase 154 acres on the Russian River, south of Ukiah. They called their village Yokayo. Charlie Pinto, Joseppa's father, was one of the group's lead-ers. The Pomo of Yokayo adopted the dress, architecture, and implements of the settler culture. They planted grain and hops; they built barns, hop kilns, houses, and a large "round house"—all of sawmill lumber. But they retained their own language and traditions, including basketmaking, which Joseppa probably learned as a child from her mother, Mary Pinto, a skilled basketmaker. Joseppa left Yokayo sometime in the early 1880s. She returned to Yokayo with her infant son, Billy, and married Jeff Dick in the mid-1880s. Together they built a modern house and established a successful farm. During the winter months Joseppa, like other Pomo women, made baskets. The women would gather in small circles, sitting on the ground with their awls and basket materials, gossiping and joking as they worked.[8]

Joseppa soon gained a reputation among the Pomo women and among traders as an expert basketmaker. She made baskets with tight, even weaving, exquisite designs, and careful construction. In 1892 Henry Henshaw photographed her in front of her Euro-American style house at Yokayo Rancheria with Jeff and Billy. She was weaving an oblong, or canoe, basket. Joseppa's baskets were already much in demand by collectors. She took orders for them months in advance. The growing scarcity of woodpecker feathers and the care with which Joseppa worked sometimes delayed completion for years. By the turn of the century the Dick family was among the wealthiest and most successful at the rancheria. Joseppa's art and industry helped the family build a comfortable wooden house, to purchase household commodities, and to assume an outward culture that differed little from their Anglo neighbors. Joseppa's house also served as her studio, the place where she stored her baskets, beads, feathers, and materials for coiling.[9]

In 1903 the Dicks went to Albuquerque at the invitation of Fred Harvey, who began a chain of dining and lunch rooms, and hotels, along the Santa Fe Railroad in 1876. He operated curio shops in many of his hotels and hired Indians to demonstrate their artisanal skills. Many worked at his establishment in Albuquerque. The Dicks stayed in Albuquerque for three months, made fifty cents a day, and sold all their products to the Harveys. By December 1903 they were back at Yokayo. Although dealers still used Joseppa's work as a standard against which to evaluate the work of other basketmakers, she produced only a few more baskets. By 1904 Joseppa and Jeff were increasingly at odds with their Yokayo community, partly because the couple did not share

their prosperity in the community and partly because of Jeff's involve-
ment in the murder of another Pomo man, for which he was convicted
and imprisoned. Joseppa narrowly escaped conviction as an accessory
and moved away from Yokayo to live on a neighboring ranch. She died
alone and isolated from her former friends in October 1905.[10]

Grace Hudson, who painted Joseppa in 1898 at the beginning of her
own career, sketched another picture of her in 1933, twenty-eight years
after Joseppa's death. The second picture of Joseppa was a portrait probably
done from an earlier sketch completed before Joseppa died. The 1933 portrait shows Joseppa's strong face burdened with sadness. There is an understanding in that powerful portrait of all that Joseppa had survived. Grace
photographed this second picture of Joseppa and numbered it 663, but she
did not sell it. She gave this special portrait to John.[11]

Standing at a graveside destroying exquisite baskets; photograph-
ing and numbering works of art. The two images seem quite different.
Grace was a descendant of the settler culture that had dispossessed
the Native American Pomo women. But like Joseppa she practiced
her art in a new cultural context, while maintaining part of the old.

Grace Carpenter was born in 1865, about five years after Joseppa,
and spent the first four years of her life in Potter Valley, north of Ukiah
in Mendocino County, California. Grace's mother, Helen Carpenter,
left one of the best-known travel accounts of westering Euro-American women. It began: "Ho! for California. At last we are on our way...
with a little good luck we may someday reach the 'promised land.'"
Helen's first child was born in Grass Valley, where the family broke its
trip from Kansas. After nineteen months the family moved on to Potter Valley to rejoin family and friends. There Helen taught school and
cared for the children and the farm, while her husband left to get newspaper work in Ukiah to add to the family's income.[12]

Potter Valley, the "promised land" for the Carpenters, was part of
the lands taken from the Pomo by the U.S. government and opened to
Euro-American settlers. The settlers brought disease and destroyed the
wild food supply of the Pomos. Some of the Euro-American women
attempted to ameliorate conditions with gifts of food and doctoring,
but they could do little to lessen the disaster to which they contributed
with their presence. It was a harsh meeting of cultures.

In 1869 the Carpenter family moved to the new village of Ukiah
where business contacts offered greater economic opportunities. The

Carpenters, like other settlers, scrambled for money. Grace's father became a county deputy assessor, continued to work occasionally in San Francisco, and opened a photography studio. Grace helped her father in his studio and at thirteen was sent off to Normal School in San Francisco. During the summers she hand-colored photographs in her father's studio. In 1880, at age fifteen, she began study at the California School of Design, the finest art school in the West.[13]

Grace was not venturing into a bastion of male tradition by receiving training at the California School of Design. Art training for women had changed drastically during the 1870s and Grace was able to take advantage of these changes. Grace received some training from her parents, a traditional way for women to learn art, from kin. During the earlier nineteenth century, a women's decorative arts movement had provided leadership in folk arts and in nonacademic art. Most early nineteenth-century training came from self-study or apprenticeship to kin, and then increasingly with artists who began to accept women as students in their studios, perhaps because the growing number of male artists needed students as a source of income.[14]

The West seems not to have been unique in establishing art schools that welcomed women in the 1870s. The California School of Design opened in San Francisco in 1874, the New York Art Student's League the following year. Both accepted women who soon became the majority of students. When the California School of Design opened, forty-six of the first class of sixty were women. Women flocked into these art schools because their opportunities for art study still remained more limited than those for men and because a women's art movement had made art a respectable occupation for women and offered them group support. In San Francisco, women exhibited regularly and had their own all-women exhibits and art clubs. The school hired women as faculty. No one could maintain that art training was denied to young women in this western culture. Acceptance of women in the professional art world did mean that women would increasingly depend on male mentors to succeed in the system, because males controlled the rewards that determined who would become the leading artists.[15]

By the 1880s Grace was joining many women in choosing art as a profession. The 1890 census listed eleven hundred women artists and art teachers active in the West. Some of these women artists were achieving regional and even national recognition. Women artists had already created quite a body of work in the West. Mary Elizabeth Michael Achey used oils, watercolors, pen and ink, and pencil in the 1860s to depict western scenes in California and other states. In the 1870s Helen Tanner Brodt painted buildings, landscapes, ranch scenes and missions in northern California, while Constance Frederica Gordon-Cumming painted watercolors in Yosemite. During the 1880s Matilda Lotz became well known; Edith White was already sketching California landscapes; and Mary Hallock Foote established a national reputation as an illustrator of western themes, many from California. Helen Henderson Chain was painting landscapes and pueblo scenes in California.[16]

Despite the artistic work of Anglo-American women in the 1880s, becoming a professional artist was still hard and remaining a professional after marriage was even harder. The Anglo-American tradition valued a woman's private virtues and performance over a public career as an artist.

Exactly how Grace dealt with this problem is difficult to know. Perhaps her parents did not really consider that she could have a career painting, but neither did they approve of her decision, at nineteen, to marry a man of thirty-three. During fifteen months of unhappy marriage Grace quit painting. But by 1889, after her divorce, she had a studio and was painting again. Then she met John Hudson, a medical doctor who opened his practice in Ukiah. He encouraged her to continue painting after they married in 1890. For the next four decades John Hudson provided the male mentorship Grace needed to fashion a career as a successful woman artist. Her success, in turn, allowed John to retire from his medical practice to become a basket collector and amateur ethnologist among the Pomo, as well as her agent. John apparently persuaded Grace to focus almost entirely on the Pomo people in her paintings.[17]

Within two years of their marriage, John was arranging to exhibit Grace's pictures. He showed them in San Francisco at the Art Association and the Mechanic's Fair, in Washington at the Smithsonian, in Chicago at the 1893 Exposition, and at exhibits in Minnesota.

Grace achieved her first popular success exhibiting pictures of Pomo babies. Babies were a popular subject for women painters at the time. Grace began to number her paintings in 1891. Her numbered paintings include a few studies of young women and one older

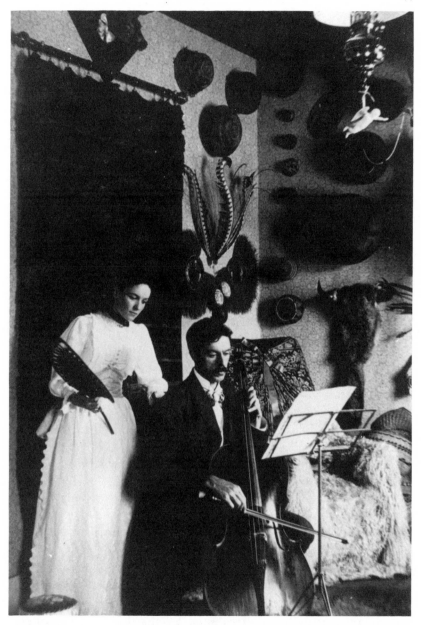

Grace and John Hudson at home, 1890. Courtesy Grace Hudson Museum.

man between 1892 and 1900, but most of these works portray chubby
Pomo babies.[18]

By 1893 John was not just exhibiting her pictures but managing
her career as well. John offered advice in his letters to her when she
went to San Francisco to show her own paintings. "Make friends all
you can...don't sell your talent too cheap....There is *prestige* in big
high prices....Don't let any conceited fool touch your picture with a
brush....Be sure of your company for many see you." John helped Grace
write descriptions of Pomo rituals, beliefs, and values to accompany
the paintings.[19]

By the end of 1893 the shrewd marketing had paid off. Grace
had sold her first baby pictures and her work was shown in a New
York illustrated art journal. John quit his medical practice in 1895
to devote full time to his own collecting and selling. During a
trip to New York that year, John sized up the eastern art market
and decided Grace could sell her paintings for more in the West.
In New York, John saw celebrated names on small canvases selling for under one hundred dollars. Grace's paintings were already
selling for well over one hundred dollars, and one placed in a
London gallery was priced at eleven hundred dollars. Between
May 1893 and May 1895 Grace painted some forty pictures,
mostly of Pomo babies, and they sold nearly as fast as she finished them for increasingly larger sums.[20]

John's aggressive marketing, however, was having a disastrous effect on Grace. Apparently she wanted to go to Paris to continue her
training, but John discouraged it. One young artist had come back and
disappointed her friends, he wrote to her in 1895: "I am almost convinced that Paris would do the same for you, for unless genius is invin-
cible against a Master's teaching the pupil will never be more than a
copyist and a 2d or 3d rate one." John may have been right; nevertheless, Grace wanted and needed time to think about the direction of
her work. She was showing her work throughout the United States—
in New York, Denver, Washington, D.C., Chicago, and Cincinnati. In
1900 she exhibited her work at the Paris Exposition. Finally, exhausted
with the pressure to produce for the market that John had helped create, she insisted on going off alone. In early 1901 she left for Hawaii for
an extended stay to rest and to practice her art in a new environ-

ment. John, meanwhile, went off to collect for the Chicago Field Museum.[21]

The few surviving letters from Grace show that she was exhausted. "Both mentally and physically I was nearer a collapse than I had supposed," she wrote. In February she tried to paint but was still too tired and put away her brushes. Later in the month she wrote, "I feel as though I never want to paint again. I hate the sight of my brushes." In March she did begin to paint again but she was ashamed of the result and worn out with the effort. "My working brain is still weary," she wrote to John.[22]

Not only Grace's painting but her relationship with John seems to have reached a crisis. He wrote anxiously to her on their eleventh wedding anniversary, April 30, 1901, criticizing his own "want of affection or its exhibition, my indifference to the future and want of energy to reach an ideal for both of us." He was, however, now happy in his work and looked back on medicine as "a master I secretly abhorred and had not the courage to leave." The money she had saved and future sales should be enough to supply her with pin money. He wrote, "I don't want you to quit painting, but it should be not for revenue only but for the honor." He kept up his advice by mail: "Keep your sketches and photos especially of the nude.... A 'Hula' dancer in ancient dress, half life at least, would stir the souls and purses, at least the tongues." It was during her absence in Hawaii that John sold Grace's first picture of Joseppa for five hundred dollars.[23]

During her stay in Hawaii Grace seems to have been the closest to moving on to her own separate life as an artist. Whatever Grace wrote in return to John, he became increasingly concerned. When she wrote to him in May that she planned to stay longer in Hawaii, he replied in great alarm: "No remorse in after life could console me for willingly leaving my wife in a distant country practically alone for a long period and the barest chance of her leaving a taint behind her. You are not a 'new woman.' God forbid such to me as companion and a real woman is the most susceptible of injury when absent from her natural lover and protector."[24]

But Grace seemed to be getting along fine. Despite John's attempt to control her from afar, she continued to do just as she pleased in Hawaii. A June article in the *Pacific Commercial Advertiser* said she would stay indefinitely, was painting Hawaiian, Japanese, and Chinese children in Honolulu, and was going to Hilo on the Big Island. Grace spent a month in Hilo sketching, then returned to Honolulu and began to complete the sketches in oils. By autumn Grace had completed twenty-seven paintings. The majority of these paintings were of children, but one was the extraordinary *Old Hawaiian Woman,* which she also kept for John. She was enjoying her work and her new friends.[25]

John thought she was enjoying her work and her new friends too much. Early in September he wrote jauntily from Fresno, "Your time is up, my girl—Come home!" John planned to go east and wanted her to accompany him. When she did not appear, he wrote more peremptorily: "If we are to live together again it must commence within a week or two of your receiving this letter." He was annoyed that it did not suit her to return and complained that her sole excuse was "you wish to exhibit some of your painting and must be present during that period and the length of which I haven't the least idea."[26]

Despite his angry words, John waited for Grace. She returned to San Francisco on November 16, 1901, with her paintings and two days later they left for Chicago. When they returned in May 1902, Grace turned again to her painting, but at a more relaxed pace. She accompanied John on some of his anthropological field trips and painted fewer pictures.

Grace seems also to have achieved a more settled relationship with her Pomo models after she returned in 1901. At first that relationship was discordant. Because Pomos did not have a figurative tradition in their art, most did not want to be photographed or to be represented in paintings. They also did not trust settlers. Although Grace grew up in areas where the Pomo were a daily presence, the two cultures did not mix easily. The Pomo had good reason to distrust settlers. First Mexicans and then Americans captured adults and children. After Pomos killed two particularly abusive Anglo ranchers in 1850, the American cavalry massacred one fishing village at Clear Lake; kidnapping of children continued into the 1870s. By the early 1890s Pomos were willing to work for Anglo settlers, but they continued to observe their traditions that forbade representations in art. Grace could not get anyone to pose for her.[27]

To get her first Pomo models, Grace manipulated Indian women to get access to their children. Mothers brought their children with them when they worked. Grace would hire the mother, then arrange some disturbance so that the mother gratefully allowed her to care for the child. Then she surreptitiously painted the little one. Grace wanted to paint their expressions, but Pomo children seldom exhibited emotion and Grace had to extort expressions. "I worried, tormented, bullied and frightened the one poor little fellow for two days, trying to make him cry....I grew ashamed of myself and gave it up," Grace once said. Pomo mothers must have known about her tactics because they seldom returned. Grace complained that she had to use different children for a single painting.[28]

Gradually, Grace established friendships that allowed her greater access to models. A young woman, Katum, and Captain John Mewhinney, an older man she had known since her youth, allowed her to paint them in 1892. In 1895 Rosa Peters posed for her. Rosa and Grace became friends, and over the next twenty years Rosa and her family posed for some thirty canvases. In 1896 Grace met Tom Mitchell; he and his family eventually appeared in more than one hundred paintings. And Joseppa agreed to pose in 1898.[29]

By the turn of the century, Grace had plenty of models who came to her Ukiah studio. She used the models primarily for facial expressions. Then she added Pomo baskets and other material objects at her studio or from John's collection. Finally, she used sketches made in the rancherias and outdoors for the backgrounds. Young men seldom modeled for her. Either she did not seek them out or they were less willing to dress as "natives." Most of her paintings were of children, young women, or elders who may have seemed less threatening to both her and her audiences.

Grace continued to paint Pomo babies—she never had children of her own—but over the years she painted more pictures of older Pomo women and men. Her most powerful paintings and drawings are of Pomo women, whom she painted with respect—Joseppa and her mother, Mary Pinto; "The Kol-pi-ta," last of the medicine women; "The Ki-me-ya," last tribal singer; and "The Bu-ta-Madtha," Bear Woman whose task was to destroy enemies. *Bear Woman*, painted in 1920, steadily returns the gaze of the viewer. In these paintings the women cease to be merely objects. They are people of power and dignity.

After the Hawaii trip Grace stayed home or traveled with John. As her work became well known, she depended less on John and increasingly on galleries to market paintings. Formal contracts regulated these professional relationships. John sold his collection of baskets to the

Smithsonian in 1899. They built Sun House in 1911 where the two lived until John died in 1936. Grace died the following year. Sun House in Ukiah was joined by the Grace Hudson Museum in 1986.

With both Joseppa and Grace, one is struck by their ability to expand out of supportive frontier cultures to produce marketable art. Yet both women reintegrated themselves into their cultures at moments of crisis, demonstrating a need for those supportive cultures. Emma Freeman also practiced her art in northern California, but moved away from traditional Anglo culture and attempted to create a new space where she could practice her art and work with Native American women as well. Like Grace Carpenter, Emma Freeman tried to carve out an artistic career in postfrontier California. But whereas Grace worried that the public considered photography an art inferior to painting, Freeman was eager to experiment with it.

Freeman was not alone in her interest. In the West large numbers of women participated and excelled in photography. Peter Palmquist, a photographic historian, estimates that in California alone more than seven hundred women were involved in some aspect of photography before 1903. Mary Alice Keatinge wrote about a three-hundred-mile photography expedition she and a friend took in California in May 1903 "to take advantage of the independence that California offers to women who would tour alone over her mountains and valleys." Other women toured with their husbands. Maude Wilson had a studio at Carmel where she did portraits of tourists for profit and lyric landscapes for pleasure. Annie W. Brigman made radically new studies of nudes in natural surroundings. By 1913 Imogen Cunningham had already made a reputation at her studio in Seattle and was preaching photography as an ideal profession for women. Dorothea Lange and Laura Gilpin were beginning their work. Freeman turned to the landscape around Eureka and to the nearby Indians of Humboldt County. Some of Freeman's photographs, like some of Hudson's paintings, objectified and romanticized Indians. But she was resourceful, humorous, and she worked with Yurok and Hoopa women at a sort of joint imaging of Native Americans. Through pictures they manipulated the nostalgia of Anglo-Americans for the past. They were not only part of the West but also part of fantasizing it.[30]

Nebraska was the birthplace of Emma Richart in 1880. Years later she wrote of herself as a Nebraska farm girl who at the age of eight swore to become an artist, made drawings of her teacher on the black-board, and drew with a prized ten-cent box of crayons. She dreamed of San Francisco, saved her egg money, and made it to Denver where she sold ribbon flowers and a few sketches, then married Edwin Freeman, a salesman, when she was twenty-two. Ed's savings and occasional employment brought them to San Francisco.[31]

In 1904 San Francisco already had many eastern tourists searching for mementoes they could take home with them to remember their trip "West." Emma began to create and furnish dealers with hand-crafted curios, small novelties of leather and wood, hand-colored photographs and sketches in pastel and watercolor. Soon her crafts were so popular that the couple opened their own stationer's shop where she could sell her handcrafts directly. Before long, Emma had met other artists and art students who urged her to get formal art training. She did so, taking private lessons with a noted and popular landscape artist, Giuseppe Cadenasso. Emma devoted herself seriously to painting and drawing for two years. Then, Emma recalled, "came the San Francisco fire and a fresh start on a borrowed hundred dollars capital in the city of Eureka. There the little San Francisco art shop was duplicated."[32]

Eureka, the largest town in California north of San Francisco, was located on Humboldt Bay, three hundred miles from the city that had nurtured Emma's desire to become an artist and one hundred miles south of the Oregon border. The Euro-American population at the time was eight thousand. The year before Emma arrived, mobs of men had driven out all the Chinese. Most Indians lived in their own communities. The small town was the commercial center of this area. At first, the Freemans sold out of their home. By 1908 they had purchased a downtown store. Ed Freeman flourished in the small coastal lumbering town. He joined a quartet, learned commercial photography, and took his camera on long photographic excursions. He loved camping with his male cronies and seemed content in the small town.[33]

Emma apparently was not so content. She wanted to return to San Francisco and resume her art studies. But Ed's success held them there and the automobile began to bring increasing numbers of tourists to their downtown store. Emma took over the main management of the store and found a landscape artist with whom to continue her art lessons. She began to turn the small shop into a gallery selling paintings and drawings by local artists, mostly landscapes of the redwoods and the coast.[34]

Emma Freeman, Courtesy The Edward E. Ayer Collection, The Newberry Library.

In 1910 a purchase by the Freemans of the camera and studio equipment of a Eureka photographer changed Emma's life. Experimenting
with the new equipment, she began to explore artistic portraiture.
Emma's romantic portraits soon became very popular. She began to
photograph landscapes and, with Ed gone most of the time, moved
into the store to live.[35]

By 1913 Emma was feeling successful but still restless. In July the
former governor of Illinois lectured for the local chautauqua and when
he impulsively asked her to ride with him to San Francisco she impulsively said yes. They arrived in the late morning, had lunch, and he left
for Chicago. Emma stayed on in San Francisco, going to the theater to
see "Everywoman," a play she wrote Ed every woman ought to see,
visiting her old art instructor and his family, and seeing friends. Emma
was feeling as liberated as Grace must have on her trip to Hawaii, but
Ed was less patient than John.[36]

Ed was also unable to tolerate the publicity when Emma's trip turned
into a public rather than just a private adventure. When newsmen asked
Ed if Emma had *his* permission to go to San Francisco, he answered no
and went to see his attorney about a separation. Ed claimed adultery in
his suit for divorce, but Emma denied the charges and stayed in the
community, becoming the sole proprietor of the Freeman Art Company. She carried on her work as a successful—though now divorced—
businesswoman and artist. Free of a husband who was no longer helpful
to her personally or professionally, Emma joined the increasing number of divorced career women in California. The public seemed more
willing to accept Emma as a divorced woman than as a wife whose
sexuality they still expected to closely monitor. Emma now began
to shape her own art and life style. She began to call herself the
founder and proprietor of Freeman Art, a student of birds and flowers, sky and clouds who had selected Humboldt County to develop
her talent for drawing, painting, and photography, who became "a
true lover of nature and an expert in photography." She claimed the
title of "artist with the camera."[37]

As Emma and her company prospered, friends began to congregate
at the shop. Among Emma's new friends were a number of Indians
who directly influenced her work, young people with Indian mothers
and Anglo fathers, many of whom had attended local government
Indian schools or the Carlisle Indian School in Pennsylvania. Emma

encouraged these young people to value their mothers' cultures. One of her friends was Bertha Thompson, the daughter of a Yurok woman and an Anglo timberman. Bertha's mother, Lucy Thompson, actively participated in Yurok culture, maintained a collection of garments and baskets, and in 1916 published an account of her life. Bertha graduated from public school, trained as a nurse in San Francisco, and returned to Eureka to work. Bertha learned to make carefully crafted baskets and sold them through Emma's store. Bertha and Emma collaborated in a series of posed pictures and photographed nature with Bertha in the foreground as a small figure. Bertha also gave demonstrations of basket weaving at the store.[38]

A second friend, Bertha Stevens, like Bertha Thompson was bicultural. Her mother was also Yurok, her father an Anglo miner. Stevens attended Carlisle and majored in home economics. Emma hired her to retouch photographs and Bertha Stevens soon moved in with Emma. Later she married Emma's male photographic assistant. Stevens reminisced later: "We had great fun. Emma dressed in an eccentric manner, sometimes with boots and a man's hat with rattlesnake skin around its crown. I made her a tailored suit which she was very happy [with]… she liked to experiment and had very odd… nocturnal work habits, often working all night, or getting up at 3 A.M."[39]

Stevens tolerated minor changes in Emma's Indian portraits. Emma frequently put a feather and headband on Yurok and Hoopa women in her photographs though they never wore them. But Bertha Stevens urged Emma not to mix the material culture of one tribe with that of another and objected strenuously when Emma photographed a woman with a warrior's bows and arrows. Other Indian friends whom Emma photographed always insisted on absolutely accurate dress and objects. Her Indian friends thus participated in the creation of images and their control.[40]

Eventually Emma had two hundred photographs in her northern California series on Indians. Freeman identified some of her most idealized, heroic subjects as being of "blended blood." Several studio photographs are stunningly simple and beautiful representations of older Indian women in Euro-American dress with traditional native hats and necklaces.

Emma sold her business in 1919 and returned to San Francisco. Success did not follow her. Photographic competition among the ninety studios was fierce and almost fifty stores also sold art supplies. Indian artifacts, photographs, and paintings were less popular after World War I. Within two years the business had failed. Emma gave up a more modest second art goods shop in 1925 and married. Two years later, at forty-eight, she died of a stroke.

At their best, Freeman's photographs depict dignified Native American women and men in portraits, natural settings, or in their daily lives. At their worst, they create a fantasy life, objectifying women, often in ways that could only have been aimed at the male viewer. Had Freeman operated within an artistic tradition and with better training, as Gilpin and Lange did later, she might have been able to create a larger body of work that more nearly conveyed the lives of the different cultures and peoples of northern California. Instead she participated in the packaging and selling of Indian culture. Nevertheless Freeman was a part of the postfrontier culture. She did not just move through the landscape "Kodaking the Indians." She lived with, laughed with, and enjoyed the American Indian women she knew. They arrived by different paths at a postfrontier culture not knowing where to go next. To go back to a traditional life was as impossible for Freeman as it was for Bertha Thompson and Bertha Stevens, who as American Indians could no longer find a place for themselves at the center of a culture. For a moment in the Freeman studios perhaps they found a common ground, a space where cultures could be shared and a new one created.

These three artists—Joseppa Dick, Grace Hudson, and Emma Freeman—illustrate how successful women artists could be in postfrontier cultures. For each of these women, significant others—mothers, fathers, mentors, husbands, and friends—were crucial. Both Joseppa and Grace had strong fathers and mothers. Both received careful training in their art, Joseppa from her mother who was an outstanding artist herself, Grace from the best art school in the West. Emma, with limited art training, experimented in a form of artistic expression that was not dependent upon extensive formal training to produce a salable product. Joseppa and Grace had partners who took an interest in their art. All three women had considerable financial success. To be creative, all women had to devote large amounts of time to their own work, to give it primacy, and to control it. Both Joseppa and Grace managed to involve their husbands in their work in supportive ways. When Emma could not maintain that support, she arranged for her own supportive network of friends. The creative woman needed a nurturing partner and nurturing friends.[41]

These three women artists of northern California each left an impressive body of creative work. Their lives demonstrate that women could maintain the support they needed as artists to achieve public recognition and a measure of financial success in postfrontier cultures. Behind the success of these three women lay cultural traditions that enabled them to participate in the creation of a new western culture. Their energy remains, embedded in the art they created.

3

NAMING A PRICE, FINDING A SPACE
THE MARKETPLACE

Last summer I drifted along with my partner to take a look at the telescopes atop Kitt Peak near Tucson, Arizona. Not really interested in the technical side of telescopes, I wandered into the museum and gift store. I expected the usual star charts, planet pictures, postcards of telescopes perched on mountains. Just inside the door I stopped. There, set out in cabinets and on long shelves, were hundreds of baskets. Some were at least thirty inches across, flaring out roundly with green patterns on creamy beige yucca. Others were miniatures with tiny stitches. Each had a small card attached identifying the artist, usually a woman. Later, a tour guide picked up a small, gently flared brown-and-buff bowl and explained. Astronomers had found the perfect mountain at Kitt Peak. But it belonged to the Tohono O'odham, who agreed to lease the mountaintop to the astronomers only if they contracted to sell always the wares of the basketmakers. And they do, in large quantities.

During the 1920s and 1930s major highways were built across the Southwest and along the coast. Where these main roads crossed Indian lands, basketmakers adapted to the new trade with the motoring public. The basket trade flourished, especially where alternative wage work was not readily available, where cultural survival seemed less threatened and less dependent on keeping baskets within the group, where Indians had no access to other markets, and where plentiful supplies of inexpensive materials existed.[1]

Developing a trade in southwest basketry, like that in pottery, was part of the combined efforts of Indian women and Anglos. The women wanted to maintain their arts as sources of income and artistic enjoyment. Anglo merchants and businesspeople wanted to develop Indian arts as tourist attractions. Indian women in some regions had no access to markets and thus gradually reduced their production for trade. Others, like the Pomo, continued to find a ready market for their baskets during the first two decades of the twentieth century. Anglos from the East had access to eastern markets through shipping and tourism. When the Atcheson, Topeka, and Santa Fe Railway and the Fred Harvey Company launched their Indian Detours (tours by automobile to Indian villages from the railway station near Santa Fe) in 1926, they ensured that baskets of some Indian cultures survived as arts, even though the interest of the eastern elite in American antiquities seemed to decline.[2]

The middle-class took up touring by auto with enthusiasm. By train and by car, travelers crossed the country, stopping to buy Indian art along with food, gas, and lodging. And they continued to do so right through the Great Depression. Roads remained so poor that as late as the 1940s, tourists still joked that Albuquerque kept its highways in disrepair purposely so businesspeople could keep tourists in town overnight. Nevertheless, public works paved hundreds of miles of the first interstate highway system in the 1930s and many middle-class families used them. I still have a vivid memory of driving from California to the Midwest hinterland, when the miles seemed interminable. By the side of the road stood the Indian women in their traditional dress, with small painted pots and woven trays. Somehow we convinced my father to stop briefly while we bought a pot or a tray for a dollar before speeding on across the desert.

Most of us probably have some such benign memories of the marketplace, but the marketplace can be a powerful shaper of creativity. In the 1930s it could provide Pueblo women with one dollar spent by tourists for a pot or provide Georgia O'Keeffe with thousands of dollars paid by collectors for small paintings. The market could pay writers like Mary Austin $8.75 in royalties for the hundreds of hours she spent creating a book or it could pay Zoë Akins $75,000 for the movie rights to her Pulitzer Prize–winning play The Old Maid. Driven sometimes by consumers who valued art for the pleasure it brought, sometimes by the status it conveyed, and often mediated by those who bought cheap and sold dear, the marketplace, by the 1930s, could be a ruthless part of an acquisitive, profit-oriented economy dominated by people who had the skills to manipulate it. In the 1920s and 1930s the market rewarded some western women handsomely for their work, and some shabbily.

Native American women of California were among the first to be affected by the increased market for baskets. Many people profited from their art. Trade began in the nineteenth century with a local market, where women sold or bartered their baskets directly to settlers for services or commodities. It ended in the twentieth century with a scramble by dealers to monopolize the output of basketmakers and to sell baskets on the national market for great profits. Not all Anglo dealers were rapacious profitmakers. Many also wanted to preserve the best of the art that basketmakers created and lodge it safely in collections where it could be studied and appreciated. But their buying frenzy coincided with other events. Postfrontier settlers and governments degraded the environment that provided the materials for California basketmakers. Settlers and governments also denigrated the artistic traditions of the women and tried to interfere with their ability to pass on those traditions to younger women. Finally, dealers discouraged the women from entering into and controlling the art market themselves. Some Indian women in California withdrew almost entirely from the marketplace, choosing to keep the declining supply of baskets within their cultures and their homes where they were used to maintain an artistic tradition among native women.[3]

The market in baskets of the northern California Pomo shared some of the ruthless characteristics of markets for indigenous art elsewhere. Many traders simply stole the art when they could, especially funereal art. When Pomos burned their dead and destroyed art to honor them, robbing graves was not generally rewarding. But as Pomos adopted Christian burial rites, the temptation to rob graves of funereal art increased. Grace Nicholson, a Pasadena trader, reported in 1906 that grave robbers stole the bodies of one man's mother, father, and sister and the people were much "exercised." John Hudson, husband of the artist Grace Hudson, sometimes complained about the tactics of other collectors, but admitted his own ruthlessness in one letter to Grace. "I robbed some half dozen granddaddy graves and am strongly advised to skip before the bucks hear of it," he wrote to his wife while on a collecting trip in 1901. Hudson sometimes posed as a casual traveler uninterested in the art. "This scheme finally fetched them and when the market finally broke I was offered all kinds of things at reasonable prices... from 60 cts to $3.00 ," he wrote proudly to Grace.[4]

Indians guarded their burial grounds as carefully as possible to secure their ancestors against depredations, and the women quickly
learned how to bargain in the new Anglo marketplace. White collectors also learned very quickly that they must negotiate a price if they
wished to establish a market. A trader on one reservation who took
whatever he could find and threw money on the ground instead of
bargaining and respectfully passing money by hand was promptly ejected
by the Indians.[5]

Such violation of elementary trading customs could endanger the
market for all. Most traders learned to conform to the Indian custom of
bargaining. Women put a value on the baskets for their own internal
trade. They knew who were the best basketmakers and who had produced a particularly beautiful work of art.[6]

Women monitored collectors as best they could. When John
Hudson was collecting baskets and basket materials for the 1893 exhi-
bitions in Chicago and San Francisco, two women trailed him to the
express office demanding to know where he was going with a package.
He was shipping one of his wife's paintings, but Indians believed he was
sending baskets back East to make a lot of money. They had read in the
local paper that John was collecting for the exposition and were aware
that collectors would wait until Indians were short of funds in the winter to make their buying trips. Hudson himself referred to this type of
buying as a "raid" and timed his own buying trips to coincide with hard
times. He tried to establish a monopoly over certain areas, buying low
in the hinterland and selling high on the San Francisco art market.
Other buyers traveled great distances and endured inland summer heat
to buy baskets. Grace Nicholson, the Pasadena dealer, sometimes hired
a boat to buy from Indians in villages along rivers.[7]

The Pomo had the additional problem of declining supplies of
basketmaking materials, which began in the nineteenth century when
Anglo settlers arrived and increased in the early twentieth century.
Indians carefully maintained supplies of sedge roots through weeding
and burning of competing growth, as well as other agricultural techniques. Private property holders gradually excluded them from the best
sources of sedge roots, forestry controls prevented burning, and maintaining the supply of the best weaving materials became difficult. They
had to go great distances to obtain good material.[8]

As basketmaking materials disappeared from the environment, artists tried to obtain alternatives. When quail feathers became scarce, for

example, basketmakers asked buyers to purchase feathers for them. As fewer women produced baskets for the market, some negotiated long-term contracts, offering their entire output in return for a regular, agreed upon sum. Joseppa Dick put her work on the open market. Mary Benson, another fine Pomo basketmaker, contracted to sell Grace Nicholson all her baskets. Fine basketweaving was exacting, time consuming work that brought little financial return. As alternative sources of cash became available—especially as hop growing developed in the Pomo country and workers could pick hops for cash—women spent less time basketmaking for the market. No regular tourist trade seems to have developed in the Ukiah Valley to bring retail buyers to the region in large numbers.[9]

The best Pomo basketweavers still taught their young daughters, granddaughters, and nieces to weave. But as the number of basketmakers declined and as cash incomes became available, most women preferred not to sell their baskets. Elsie Allen, a great basketmaker who died in 1990 at the age of ninety, described her basketmaking career in the 1920s in such a way. As a child Allen learned basketmaking from her mother and her grandmother and helped them gather sedge roots, willows, redbuds, and bulrushes. She went off to school, then to work in San Francisco, married in Ukiah, and raised a family. She began to make baskets in the early 1920s but buried them with relatives—her grandmother, a great uncle, a brother-in-law. She also loaned baskets to other Pomos for rituals that did not require that baskets be buried with the dead. They then returned the baskets to her.[10]

The decline of California baskets can best be traced through the basket business of Grace Nicholson, the Pasadena trader who built a modest fortune on the sales of her baskets in the early decades of the twentieth century. Nicholson arrived in Pasadena late in 1901, partly to find health and partly to find adventure in the West. She had a little money and a few skills. Grace had completed high school, worked as a stenographer, managed an amusement casino, and then received a small inheritance from her grandparents who died in 1900. She planned to support herself by typewriting. Soon after arriving in California on Christmas Day 1901, Grace saw some Indian baskets in a curio store and bought them. She then borrowed five hundred dollars—"on her face," she later told friends—and opened her first business. She maintained that business for fifty years, gradually moving from collecting baskets to Asian art objects, a shift that mirrored the decline of the basket trade. It is hard to disentangle the profit of each enterprise, but she launched the Asian trade from the profits of the basket trade, spent two hundred thousand dollars in 1931 to build the Pasadena Art Institute to house Asian art, and endowed a scholarship at Scripps, to be awarded to a female student studying art.[11]

Grace made her first buying trip in 1901 and continued to buy baskets for the next thirty years. She went directly to the Indians, going up such rivers as the Eel and the Trinity in small boats to buy from families who could only be reached by water. She purchased collections from California families who had bought baskets for small sums, bartered for them, or received them as gifts in the nineteenth century and now sold them as they increased in value. The baskets, which had become a sort of western Victoriana in middle-class homes, gradually moved on to the market as impoverished widows put them up for sale.[12]

Grace claimed to have handled twenty thousand objects by 1916, most of them baskets. One scholar estimated that much of the western material in most major museums passed through Grace's hands. The Smithsonian, the Field Columbian Museum of Chicago, and the University of Pennsylvania department of Archaeology all bought from her. Hundreds of wealthy private collectors, many of them easterners, spent thousands of dollars for examples of different forms and designs, often paying as much as three hundred to five hundred dollars for individual baskets. Middle-class tourists, who just wanted a basket as an art object for their living rooms, perhaps a Tulere bottleneck for twelve to thirty dollars, bought thousands more. Poorer travelers who were satisfied with the small basket caps of the Hupa, which she sold for one to three dollars, bought the remainder.[13]

The photographs that Nicholson took testify to the great beauty of the baskets she collected. They are objects of superb form and design. Not surprisingly, women found them particularly appealing and wished to possess them. As Rayna Green has said, bowls are a particularly female form and symbol. Baskets, like pottery, express in their roundness a powerful symbol of female art.[14]

By 1903 Grace had already begun to buy Asian art objects in anticipation of the scarcity and rising prices of the California baskets. She roamed widely up the coast and through Arizona and New Mexico. Dealers were driving up the prices of the baskets. By 1914 Grace was paying two hundred dollars each for Pomo baskets. As prices rose and

Grace Nicholson travelling up a river in northern California to buy baskets, early 1900s. Courtesy Henry E. Huntington Library and Art Gallery.

Indian art objects became scarce, Grace switched to Asian art, and by 1916, she had buyers in China and Japan. She made a purchasing trip to Asia in 1929. By that time, her collecting was almost all Asian. The only baskets she sold were those she had in stock.[15]

An exchange of letters between Grace Hudson and Grace Nicholson in 1930 confirms that not only the supply but also the demand for American Indian art as a whole declined during the early years of the Depression. In 1930 Grace Nicholson was handling some of Grace Hudson's paintings at her Pasadena store. Hudson, who was married to the trader-ethnologist John, had made her reputation as a painter of the Pomo during the postfrontier period before World War I. Hudson wrote to ask about the decline in interest in her Indian pictures. Nicholson penciled her reply at the bottom of Hudson's letter: "Customers are 'off' of Indians more and more each year, I fear. Cannot even sell a basket. No one seems to have any money except to buy autos—gas—tires and oil."[16]

The market for Hudson's work, tied as it was to the Indian market, was an indicator that customers' tastes and, therefore, the marketplace were changing. The Depression focused attention on the present, and visual representations of the nineteenth-century past seemed romantic and nostalgic to many Americans. Hudson wrote Nicholson in 1931: "In these days of 'modern art' you will not need an alibi for anything." Nicholson arranged an exhibit of Hudson's paintings in 1932 to try to boost sales. Although a hundred visitors came daily to view Hudson's paintings, they did not buy. Nicholson complained that other artists were cutting prices and art magazines reporting the good buys. "Other galleries and art dealers here and in Los Angeles are offering art objects at almost any price. Business in general is bad but I am trying to keep up my standard.... So called modern art seems to have played a villain's part for past two years," she complained.[17]

The Depression did not create the shift in the market to modern art. That had been happening for more than a decade. But 1928 and 1929 do mark a watershed of sorts among art collectors. The Depression hurt the already declining Indian art market just as the market for modern art was opening up. Modern art reduced the eastern demand for American western art both old and new. A small group of collectors and buyers continued to deal in western art, and the New Deal supported regional art in the West and among Indian tribes, but an art

fashioned more closely on contemporary European styles began to domi-
nate the New York art market. The Museum of Modern Art exhibit of
1941 *Indian Art of the United States* still defined Indian art as "primitive," but with an aesthetic affinity to modern art. During the early
1930s, as Indian art was being discovered by the New York artistic elite,
Anglo artists like Hudson suffered. So, too, did writers who had once
found an eastern market for western themes. Mary Austin was one of
the writers affected as the market for western culture declined.[18]

Austin had caught the eastern market's desire for western culture
on its upswing in the early twentieth century. The search for a literary
West of the imagination that would capture the postfrontier setting
was increasing in 1903 when Houghton Mifflin published Austin's *Land
of Little Rain* for its affluent gift market.[19]

Austin had found a congenial editor in William Booth, who had
grown up in the Santa Clara Valley and recalled it nostalgically. "It is
easy to be Greek in the California spring," he wrote to Austin. Booth
recognized the potential in Austin's writing, the "possible future of
California in literature." He saw similarity in her descriptions of the
foothills and those in classic Greek literature. He shaped the market
for her books, working the juvenile as well as adult market, and cau-
tioning her not to reproduce her stories in southwest journals because
it might hurt sales.[20]

Between 1903 and 1906 Houghton Mifflin published four of Austin's
books, printing a total of twenty-seven thousand copies, all aimed at
elite readers. Wanting to extend her readership, Austin left Houghton
Mifflin between 1906 and 1907 in search of a publisher who might
deliver her books to a broader market. When she returned to Houghton
Mifflin, the press continued to publish attractive, small editions aimed
at an elite readership. The publisher sold sixty-five hundred copies of
The Ford, but *The Trail Book*, published in 1918 with illustrations and
an attractive format, sold only twenty-nine hundred copies. The sales
did not even repay the cost of printing.[21]

Austin wanted to expand the market by trying to distribute *The
Trail Book* in rural areas, but Houghton Mifflin refused the project. Their
representative wrote: "Our own experience—and it is an experience
that we believe every trade book publisher can corroborate—is that
when a publisher goes outside the ordinary channels of book distribution, he runs up against an overwhelming inertia in regard to book

buying. Consequently, to get results on the small margin of advertising, he finds it essential to concentrate at the point of least resistance, namely in the centres where there is already a large class of habitual book buyers." In correspondence with magazine publisher James E. Watson in the early 1920s, Austin wrote of her concern with the market and her search for a new subject.[22]

Austin was publishing new books with Bobbs Merrill in Indianapolis at this time. Her correspondence with editor H. H. Howland reveals continuing problems with the market. Howland complained of the literary editors who controlled reviews and sympathized with Austin's complaints about New York hostility to new ideas and its half-baked intellectuals. Rising costs made small books, such as Austin had published earlier in the century, no longer profitable. It was just as costly to publish small books and the publisher could not charge as much. Publishing now had fixed costs. Publicity, advertising, sales, and overhead were the same, regardless of the retail price of the book.[23]

What most disappointed Bobbs Merrill were the sales figures from *Everyman's Genius*, published in 1925. Despite aggressive marketing, the company estimated it made $341 on sales. Austin made only $5.17. "What the public's going to do with any book is on the knees of the gods," the editor admitted. "We think we know how to give the book the full opportunity of exciting public interest. Our success with many books leads us to think this. But candidly that's all we can do, and the rest is up to the book and the public taste." Over at Houghton Mifflin things were not much better. In January 1928 the publisher mailed Austin a royalty check for $115.43. Neither the gods nor the public were treating her well.[24]

The postfrontier California that Austin had written of so well had disappeared by 1926 when she wrote a new preface for an American edition of *The Lands of the Sun*. Ferris Greenslet, Austin's new editor at Houghton Mifflin, asked her to soften her bitter account of "the spoiling of California" because he felt he could not enlist the support of California bookstores in selling the book if her sharp criticism were printed. Austin had written that California was now "something hardly worth describing outside a realtor's circular," the beauty of southern California "torn to tatters to make a tripper's holiday... utterly vanished ... utterly changed, so blatant and bristling with triumph from the unresisting beauty of the wild." It was all true, Greenslet admitted, and could be said in an article, but not in a book they wanted to market to Californians, even to "realtors and motion picture queens of the second generation." Austin complained, but she rewrote the preface, taking out the stinging critique.[25]

With both the California and the national culture themes dry, Austin turned to New Mexico as a last literary frontier. From 1899 to 1924 Austin had divided her time between Carmel and New York. In 1918 she began to explore Santa Fe as a promising substitute for Carmel. With a half-finished novel and some commissions for magazine articles, Austin sold her Carmel house and moved to Santa Fe. The first year did not go well. She was ill and had an operation; she misplaced the manuscript of her novel; and she lost her magazine commissions. The market had fallen out of her new venture.

Despite these setbacks, Austin began to build a ten-room adobe house in Santa Fe. It had a big library–living room with a small study adjacent to it, and next to the study her bedroom. La Casa Querida, the Beloved House, as she called it, had a yard full of bushes, flowers, and herbs. During the days, which Austin spent deep in work and thought (even if she might be watering her garden at the same time), she did not welcome visitors. But after 4 P.M., she invited friends and relatives to share her home. Or she might venture out in one of her Panama hats decorated with great blue poppies. She often took fruits, berries, and blooms when she visited friends. Writer Anne Ellis remembered Austin bringing her "homemade apple jelly and a rose geranium leaf in the glass."[26]

With La Casa Querida, Austin finally seemed content with her work and her campaigns to halt the obliteration of local cultures by Euro-Americans. In 1927 Austin objected when the Daughters of the American Revolution proposed to place one of twelve identical copies of the *Madonna of the Trail* in Santa Fe. The real pioneers were the "Spanish" people and they had not been consulted or represented, Austin declared. With the support of Austin and others, the statue went to Albuquerque. Austin learned to live as an artist without the market, nourishing her own genius during the early part of the day and encouraging the artistic work of Indian, Hispanic, and Anglo at other times.[27]

When Austin moved to Santa Fe, she was joining an Anglo arts community that was evolving an economic development policy to include Indian arts and culture. Anglo developers saw the Pueblo Indians becoming part of an aggressive national marketing plan of the Santa Fe Railroad. By 1935, in fact, the railroad's tours attracted an estimated 125,000 tourists to Santa Fe. The Pueblos had become an economic asset.[28]

Austin was successful in using her literary skills to promote Indian arts and cultures, but she was never very successful in marketing her own work from the Southwest. Nor was she as successful in her attempt to market Hispanic arts and culture. Hispanics did not turn their art into commodities as successfully as did Native Americans in the early twentieth century. Easterners accepted American Indian art as part of an exotic non-European art world by the turn of the century. Prejudice against Mexicans remained strong in the East throughout the 1930s. To claim an exotic foreign origin, Hispanas would have to be Mexican and thus face discrimination. Some began to adopt a Spanish colonial heritage during these decades in an effort to escape the problem. Others claimed Indian origin. New Mexican blankets, woven by Hispano families, had traditionally been marketed as Mexican. To avoid the cultural prejudices, a few curio dealers began to sell blankets produced in Hispano villages such as Chimayo, as Indian blankets. Although increasing numbers of Hispanas wove in families and subcontracted to weave blankets in the 1920s, marketers also emphasized the importance of male weavers. Nor did women transform colcha and crochet into salable art; it remained primarily a private household art. Hispanic arts always proved less marketable to easterners as images of the new Southwest. Low-cost Indian art provided familiar images of the Southwest and its cultures. Indian art remained the antiquity of the Americas, reminding Americans of the Indians as a noble but disappearing colonized people.[29]

Hispanic people never fit into this scheme, although Hispanic women not only created arts but also helped collect music, folklore, and stories. At the end of the 1930s a few Hispana writers—Cleofas Jaramillo, Aurora Lucero-White, Nina Otero-Warren, Fabiola Cabeza de Baca—recounted stories and recipes in books. But like Austin, these Hispanas had difficulty establishing a link between a romanticized colonial past and their current besieged culture. For Anglo, Indian, and Hispanic artists, traditionalism could paralyze creativity and stymie analysis of cultures that had been creatively changing for hundreds of years.[30]

The decade Austin spent in New Mexico was not a financial success for her. Booksellers were interested only in popular subjects, and Austin's literary interests took her down different paths. She wrote a book about death, *Experiences Facing Death,* which Bobbs Merrill reluctantly published. The press sent out announcements to one thousand reviewers. Not a single clipping was returned. Instead of the usual 15 percent spent on publicity, Bobbs Merrill spent more than 34 percent, but the book was a considerable loss. When Austin received her next royalty statement, it included $8.75 for *Everyman's Genius* and less than $60.00 for her new book on death.[31]

To supplement her meager royalties and the small advances of Houghton Mifflin, Austin continued to lecture across the country in exhausting tours that brought her small sums of money for speaking to university audiences and before civic and women's clubs. The agencies booking her lectures usually took 25 percent of fees that might amount to as little as fifty dollars. Austin felt that she never received what was her "proper estimate as a literary artist" because of the range and variety of her products—novels, essays, poems, plays, and descriptive writing—and her lack of interest in "building up a literary career." She saw her work in New Mexico as influenced by the conviction that a "great and powerful culture" would rise from the area between the Rio Grande and the Colorado. If Isadora Duncan had seen America dancing on the Rockies, Austin saw America also writing and creating visual arts.[32]

Austin's Houghton Mifflin editor finally urged her to write her autobiography. Isadora Duncan's autobiography had been selling spectacularly since its publication in 1927. The public seemed fascinated with how creative women artists described their own lives. Editors hoped Austin's autobiography might tap this market. Houghton Mifflin advanced Austin twenty-five hundred dollars so she could collect material and begin writing. Greenslet arranged for the autobiography to be a special selection for the Literary Guild, which paid six thousand dollars, nearly half of which went to cover her advance. Early in 1933 she received another three thousand dollars and in July nearly twenty-five hundred. "Taken all in all, this is a thoroughly sound sale, granted the conditions," Austin's editor assured her, "considering everything . . . I think the fact that more than four thousand copies were sold in the worst year in publishing history on top of the thirty thousand distributed by the guild makes a reasonably satisfactory showing."[33]

The time Austin spent in New Mexico—the land in which she expected to write of Indian and Hispanic cultures—resulted in very little success in the marketplace. Austin published eight new books during this decade and republished two older ones. Only one, *Starry Adventure*, dealt with New Mexico. In it, the hero grows up in New Mexico, attached to the New Mexico landscape, but he dreams of great adventure. At the novel's end he realizes that his married life in the mountains is his "starry adventure." Despite her failure in the national marketplace, Austin considered her life in New Mexico a success.[34]

Elizabeth Shepley Sergeant in a 1934 article for the *Saturday Review of Literature* perhaps best identified the problem of Santa Fe literary folk, which included Austin. Sergeant described Santa Fe as a blend of three cultures: Indian and Spanish-Mexican; Pioneer Southwest; and Colonist Southwest, from New York, Chicago, and what-not. The Colonist Southwest stretched toward Albuquerque in one direction and to Taos in the other, with Santa Fe as its literary capital. Sergeant placed Mary Austin within the scientific literary tradition, scientists "in whom the storytelling instinct ran strong [who] so generously helped to foster local arts and talents." Sergeant was sympathetic to the problems of being a Santa Fe colonial. "Such are the writers of Santa Fe whom many dangers seem to confront: the danger of provincialism or homesickness for Eastern roots—for though planes bring East and West together, writers are seldom fliers, and newspapers come late and slow—of becoming prey to the near writer and appreciative, uncritical circle that steadily grows in a place so charming to live in as this; of falling victim to the summer visitor, disrespectful of working hours; and finally of succumbing to the monumental, indifferent abundance of the land itself, with its recurrent festivals native or fabricated, its round of balls and doings, a prey to the sun, magical, restorative and indolent."[35]

I think Sergeant precisely identified the culture and the lesser problems. The greater problem was that they were colonials: they remind one of the Anglo-Indian colonial literary elite, torn between the romantic self and the exotic other, failing to understand other cultures seen only from the outside and their own culture seen only from within.

The Santa Fe colonialists, Austin included, could find a marketplace neither in the Southwest, where they spoke only to a few, nor in the New York marketplace busily contending with its own battle between romanticism and modernism. One of Austin's editors at *The Fo-*

rum, Henry Goddard Leach, described the problem quite succinctly to Austin in 1928. "When I was in New Mexico I had come from exhibits of modern art and interior decoration in New York City and I saw in the jumbled wholesale trading posts in Gallup alone the potential for a new national art that would make Paris seem futile and inane. From all I could hear or see the Navajo nations have not cracked the surface of their possibilities." Nor had Austin. But another woman artist, Georgia O'Keeffe, would be supremely successful at that task.[36]

O'Keeffe arrived in 1929 for her first summer in New Mexico with an assured New York market for her paintings. In the years between 1917, when O'Keeffe moved to New York, and her first summer in New Mexico, O'Keeffe had gone through personal and professional trials. By 1929 everyone who read the *New York Times* knew that O'Keeffe had conquered the market. For those who measured success in dollars, O'Keeffe's reputed sale of six small paintings of lilies to an anonymous collector for twenty-five thousand dollars made her the most successful painter in the country. O'Keeffe had painted about thirty paintings a year since arriving in New York a decade before. She had agreed with Alfred Stieglitz to show them only in his gallery and to allow him to decide prices and sales. Stieglitz refused at first to build up any market for O'Keeffe's paintings. Of the three hundred paintings, Stieglitz allowed only one-third, those to which he felt less attached, to be sold. Usually he set prices so outrageously above the market price that he had few purchasers.[37]

In 1926 Stieglitz was selling her paintings for higher and higher prices. Within a month after opening O'Keeffe's 1927 exhibition early in January, Stieglitz had sold at least one painting for six thousand dollars, one for three thousand, and others for one thousand dollars each. Estimates for total sales from the exhibition vary from seventeen thousand to twenty-three thousand dollars. This was the first significant income from her paintings. Then, six weeks after the exhibition closed, Stieglitz announced the sale of the lilies. It was not known until much later that this famous sale was a fabricated publicity ploy. Even without the bogus sale, by the spring of 1927 O'Keeffe knew her work could command large prices and was likely to sell well as long as she could continue to produce paintings of the same quality.[38]

Although Stieglitz successfully brokered O'Keeffe's creative output, he was not successful in protecting the source of that creativity.

Stieglitz was physically attracted to O'Keeffe as a creative artist and a woman but by the late 1920s, he had developed a sexual relationship with Dorothy Norman, a young woman who helped him run his art gallery. For Stieglitz, it seemed possible to now separate his role as agent for O'Keeffe's work from his role as husband and sexual partner. By allowing Stieglitz to join these roles, O'Keeffe had put both her personal and creative life in his management. By the time he changed his roles, O'Keeffe's self-worth as an artist and a woman had become so intertwined that the rejection by Stieglitz of O'Keeffe's sexuality threatened her creativity. Maintaining the ritual aspect of their married life, especially the summers with his family at Lake George, New York, now became stifling. Her winter painting in New York began to show a decrease in creative vitality.

O'Keeffe painted few canvases in 1928, most of them small. She began to talk and write about her desire to go West. She wrote at the time of her 1929 show: "I hope not to have an exhibition again for a long—long—long time." The catalog announced there would be none, in 1930 at least. More than one thousand visitors a week saw her 1929 show, and her paintings sold well. She had mainly to revitalize her art with the western landscape, she thought, to continue her career as a painter. "I am West again and it is as fine as I remember it," O'Keeffe wrote from Taos.[39]

The Taos artists' colony welcomed O'Keeffe. She let loose—sunbathing nude, camping out in northern New Mexico and Arizona, riding, walking, joking with the other artists and writers from the colony. Mabel Dodge Luhan's eccentricity may also have helped O'Keeffe to gain distance and perspective on her relationship with Stieglitz and his sexual liaison with Norman. At Taos O'Keeffe began to come to terms with her new situation and to devise a way to continue her relationship with Stieglitz. Mabel Dodge accepted the fact that her Taos Indian husband, Tony Luhan, had sexual relationships with other women. Mabel seemed to maintain her own self-worth despite these relationships. Perhaps O'Keeffe's friendship with and respect for Tony, as well as Mabel's determination to live her life as she wished, helped liberate O'Keeffe from her paralyzing dilemma. At least she must have begun to try on this attitude, for she told Mabel that it was a "little thing" for Tony to sleep with another woman, that they did not have the right to keep their husbands utterly to themselves. When O'Keeffe returned to

New York she seemed to be determined to continue her relationship with Stieglitz. Her paintings were revitalized as well. O'Keeffe began to work hard but slowly at painting the new western landscape.[40]

O'Keeffe's summers in New Mexico from 1929 to 1931 in no way interfered with her relationship to the New York marketplace. Stieglitz continued to handle her paintings, keeping the best and selling to a few chosen art patrons. But O'Keeffe began to assert her independence in exhibiting, lending a painting to the new Museum of Modern Art over the objection of Stieglitz. He did not expect many sales from her exhibit in February 1930, which was predominantly New Mexican paintings. But the O'Keeffe craze persisted. Critics accepted Taos as a natural extension of the New York art scene. Critic Henry McBride wrote drolly that O'Keeffe had "got religion" in Taos.[41]

In fact, summers in New Mexico, and intellectual acceptance of Stieglitz's activities were not enough to free O'Keeffe. Perhaps, they only delayed emotional resolution of the issue. Instead of going to New Mexico in the summer of 1932, she stayed in the East, continuing to sort out her relationship with both Stieglitz and the marketplace. Attempting a resolution paralyzed her nervous system so badly that it seemed her career was over. The economic depression hit her market at the same time her own depression deepened. Not one painting of her 1932 exhibit sold. Only by avoiding Stieglitz completely and concentrating on restoring her identity and self-sufficiency did O'Keeffe gradually recover her strength. A warm relationship in the winter of 1933 with Jean Toomer, the black novelist, completed O'Keeffe's restoration.[42]

She used her renewed energy to care for her creative self. "Finding my plot of earth," she called it. Reassured of her own worth as a person, she could face the marketplace again. After Toomer left, she began to paint in January 1934—the first time in fourteen months. A retrospective of her works at the Museum of Modern Art that spring did not include her New Mexico work, but it ensured her place as a preeminent modern artist. That year she returned to New Mexico. In 1935 she sought the isolation of Ghost Ranch, north of Abiquiu, and stayed for six months. That same year Elizabeth Arden salons commissioned her to paint something for their salon. Stieglitz negotiated a ten thousand dollar fee. He was setting prices of fifteen thousand dollars on other paintings. The artist had truly found her space and taken her place in the market.[43]

O'Keeffe survived in the marketplace by reconciling her personal and creative lives and remaining within the circle of Stieglitz's careful marketing techniques. She moved her art from the avant-garde to the mainstream in the late 1920s; there it remained despite a few hard years of the Depression that dragged the market down. She was able to live and work in New Mexico part of each year and to keep her place in the market. Like Austin she took long solitary walks, learned the country-side, and brought the New Mexico landscape into her art. She, more than any other Anglo artist, was able to incorporate the Southwest into modernist art.

Not a room but a house of one's own was the symbol of indepen-dence for O'Keeffe, as it had been for Austin. In 1939 she purchased and remodeled a small Ghost Ranch house on three acres of land. O'Keeffe furnished her house simply—white muslin curtains, a slab-legged plywood table, a built-in couch of adobe, lots of bones, rocks, and animal skulls. It was her own.[44]

If a house was a measure of market success, Zoë Akins' house in Pasadena, which also had three acres of land, surely placed her as one of the most financially successful western women artists. In the decade between 1929 and 1939, with her home in Pasadena serving as a base for writing both Hollywood movies and Broadway plays, Akins made nearly a million dollars.[45]

Although Akins was one of the best-known women playwrights of the early twentieth century, today she is less known than Lillian Hellman, Rachel Crothers, and Lorraine Hansberry. Akins was the only one of these women who lived most of her life in the West. She moved to California in 1907 when she was twenty-one, expecting to die there of tuberculosis. Instead, she recovered. She continued to make south-ern California her home. Her first play was produced in Los Angeles; she chose Pasadena as her permanent home; and she considered the Pasadena Playhouse to be enormously important for her success in reach-ing a mass market, which she successfully tapped first through plays, then in the 1930s through movies. She wrote more than forty plays, had nineteen produced on Broadway, and another four professionally produced elsewhere. She collaborated on dozens of films for RKO and MGM, beginning with *Sarah and Son,* the film that gave director Dor-othy Arzner her start. One author described the composite Akins woman as sophisticated, elegant, romantic, strong-willed, self-assertive, witty,

Zoë Akins, Courtesy Henry E. Huntington Library and Art Gallery.

extravagant, generous, and contradictory. Her women were, in fact, archetypal modern western women who immediately found a wide female audience in the East, first in plays, then in movies.[46]

Green Fountains, which Akins bought in 1930, was a two-story, wooden frame house built in 1894, just outside the city limits of Pasadena. It had seven fireplaces, four master bedrooms, three servant's rooms, a gardener's cottage, badminton court, and swimming pool. Zoë had a large bedroom of her own in which she wrote, and a bedroom in which she worked with her secretary, as well as a study. At the movie studio she had an office where she could write, and a studio stenographer. Akin's house had low taxes and high walls. Akins even had enough servants to provide a California upstairs-downstairs drama. She wrote to a friend: "Louise, my cook, has left me to start a restaurant. Simoncelli, the butler, went with her; Mack [the black chauffeur] has been married to a very bad mannered white girl, and my secretary has been on a three weeks' vacation." In 1932 Akins, who at forty-six was still single, married a British diplomat, Hugo Rumbold, the son of a nobleman. She brought her husband to Pasadena to live with her at Green Fountains.[47]

After Rumbold died, Akins lived on alone in the rambling California house. For more than a decade she commuted at least fifty miles a day to the movie studios in Culver City and spent months in New York working on the preparation of her plays. In 1935 she received the Pulitzer Prize for her play The Old Maid. In 1938 she sold it to Warner's Pictures for seventy-five thousand dollars.[48]

Akins worked hard to achieve her success on Broadway and in Hollywood, but her main marketing strategy was to employ an excellent agent who could find and impress producers. In April 1921, as Akins reached out for a new audience and a new style in dramatic comedy, she found in Alice Kauser an agent who would be a link between her western home and the New York marketplace. The first two years of the author-agent relationship were troublesome ones as the two women tried to shape professional relations and friendship. After a temporary break in 1923, they maintained the relationship until 1940, when Kauser died. In letters to Kauser, Akins comments about politics; she talks about difficult scenes, her money problems, her desire to write, her love of California, her hatred of the movie industry. In correspondence with Alice she developed ideas, shaped plans. Alice was the marketplace, helping her judge what would work in New York, what would not. Theirs was an extraordinary professional relationship and friendship of twenty years. Together with Akins' creativity and hard

work, the relationship enabled her to become the most financially successful woman writer of her time.[49]

Western women dealt with the market during the first half of the
century in different ways. American Indian women either withdrew
their art from the market or merchandised it for the tourist trade.
Despite the real problems that collection and tourist art presented for
Indian women, they were able to create and maintain artistic and cultural traditions. Austin, who attempted to deal with the market directly, failed to make much money from her publishing in the 1920s
and 1930s. Nevertheless, she was able to live independently, write
widely, and achieve a place as an important woman of letters and advocate for regionalism. O'Keeffe, by placing her work in the hands of a
partner with whom she had a long-term relationship, worked only when
she was able to assert her own independence. O'Keeffe survived a
major breakdown to return to painting and gain control over the distribution of her art. Finding a woman agent she trusted, and one who
understood the New York market, allowed Akins to maintain a spectacularly successful career from her Pasadena home.

Women have always had difficulty thriving in the male-dominated
market. Anglo-American women—like Hudson and O'Keeffe—have
often chosen to rely on a male mediator for the market. Men broker
their art, but the cost of that brokering may be a sexual relation that
can undercut the very energy and sense of worth that engenders their
creativity. Women mediators, such as Akins' agent, Kauser, or the communal mediators that Indian cultures sometimes provided, could offer
women attractive alternatives to this dilemma. A sustained, supportive
relationship, in whatever way it was achieved, offered a woman the
best chance to focus on her art and to receive enough material support
to maintain that focus long enough to develop her art.

These mediators or brokers must also find a supportive art world
for the women. Late nineteenth-century women who worked as visual
or literary artists often found Anglo-American women's clubs or
individual women as patrons supportive of their efforts. These patrons
sometimes provided finances for study, a market for their arts, and psychological support for their work as well. These cultural groups continued through the 1930s, but their support brought problems as well.
Volunteer cultural groups often had limited finances, superficial understanding of the arts they proposed to support, and themselves lacked

access to the male-dominated market. Moreover, after 1920 these groups lost much of their commitment to helping women. Wealthy women philanthropists either embraced a modernist aesthetic that no longer saw women's art as valuable, or applied a male-defined standard that often devalued art because it was created by women.[50]

The marketplace itself proved a fickle place for all artists. Regional art centers and literary styles provided regional markets for production both by Indian and Anglo-American women. As the modernist marketplace took form, with its centrist tendencies, it competed with regional markets to define what was worthy art. By the late 1930s modernists had embraced Indian visual arts as "primitive," therefore basically compatible with modernism. The 1941 exhibit of Indian arts at the Museum of Modern Art signaled that official view of Indian art and the end of attempts by the government to control Indian visual and performing arts.[51]

Anglo-American figurative art fared less well. While a market for figurative visual art would survive, it more often found its support among the rear guard rather than the vanguard. Private collectors continued to buy western women's art but it was western art by and about a mythic frontier peopled primarily by males. This type of western art emerged to contend for a public place in the art market during its revival in the 1960s. As the new western art museums took form they showcased the male artists who most glorified a male vision of the West.[52]

The regional literary arts that Austin had pioneered seemed hopelessly out of date on the literary markets of the 1960s that still centered in New York. Akins, the westerner who shared the fewest similarities with other regionalists, who was the most Anglophile in her sensibilities, also had trouble surviving in the postwar marketplace of the 1940s and 1950s. Her ethic seemed the least tied to regional culture because it mirrored urban (and urbane) Hollywood and New York, but it soon ceased to command the attention of the national modernist marketplace. Her letters grew more politically reactionary, racist, and anti-Semitic as she surveyed the modernist theater of the 1950s. O'Keeffe alone of the Anglo-American women considered here survived long enough to see her art undergo a revival in the marketplace of the 1970s.[53]

The Tohono O'odham basket market with which I began this chapter is the most successful of all basket markets today. Tohono O'odham produce more baskets than any other group of American

Indians in the country. They weathered hard times in the 1920s and 1930s by continuing to produce for the market. The women had few alternate incomes, and by switching from willow to Yucca they were able to make more baskets quickly. They spaced stitches further apart and designed stitching techniques that were usually interesting to non-Indians. They also experimented with nontraditional baskets, new shapes, sizes, and designs. The Tohono O'odham Council encouraged and sometimes subsidized young artists and ensured that outlets such as that at Kitt Peak were established and maintained. The basket market of the Tohono O'odham sustains artists during their early training and over long periods of time. Artists with exceptional skills emerge from this supportive culture to deal directly with the Anglo marketplace. Although Pomo basket art still survives and plays an important role in the cultural life of the Pomos, it has a much smaller place in the market.[54]

Scholars are beginning to study the market for American Indian women's arts—baskets, rugs, and pottery—in ways that address many cultural issues. Markets are constructed out of a variety of elements, of which gender is only one. Native American groups in which women created baskets did not all create lasting markets. Some, however, did find highly successful markets.

Surprisingly few theories exist about how markets are created for women in different ethnic cultures. Much discussion has been devoted to what artists do, the content of their work and, especially since the 1960s, how Anglo women have been kept from audiences. But scholars have written relatively little on how women have actually negotiated markets. Markets do affect the ability of artists to produce, and certain markets have always been responsive to some women artists. A few Anglo women artists, particularly during the modernist period from 1920 to 1945, did stunningly well. They were able to produce what the marketplace wanted and to establish the networks necessary to market their work. Women artists may have fared even better before 1920, when flourishing regional markets existed and women could move between the local and the national markets in much the way the Tohono O'odham have done more recently.[55]

Women had difficulties with the marketplace, particularly between 1945 and 1975. But some women achieved success. Scholars should devote closer analysis to the causes—geography, personal biography, community, or other factors—that permit some artists access to markets that remain closed to others. Between 1920 and 1945 some women did gain access to the major art distribution system, and some exploited the marketplace quite successfully. As the postfrontier market declined and the new modernist market became centered in New York, only a few were able to make the transition. The most successful divided their time between New York and the West, as well as having an assistant or business partner in New York to cultivate reputation and market. They also moved most successfully into modernist styles that were no longer based on exotic or specific themes, but on seemingly universal themes that subsumed the exotic within them. For Austin only her autobiography performed that role. But O'Keeffe's landscapes and Akins's comedies commanded a market that increased throughout the 1920s and 1930s. Both artists had mediators in the New York marketplace who took their work seriously, interpreted it favorably for the public, and helped create an audience for it.

Many women artists were successful during the first half of the twentieth century, although some women remained silent and others expressed their creativity only indirectly. Women, especially Anglo women, had extraordinary opportunities for creative work in the public arena. The art of some Native American women also achieved a national market.

That national market narrowed and contracted during the next twenty years, at the very time an expanded number of western women were attempting to join it. As the market narrowed, access to the historical memory of the national culture also narrowed. Western women who entered the marketplace in large numbers were invisible in the new professionalized western history. As the history of the West grew in sophistication and power—as frontier, region, urban civilization, utopia, and myth—women did not find their historians.[56] Western history was defined in a way that gave women even less space than did the marketplace. Creating a memory of their work would remain largely a task for the new historians of the West, the postmodern historians.

4

THE HUNGRY EYE
AUDIENCES

"Not to have an audience is a kind of death," western writer Tillie Olsen wrote in *Silences*. At the beginning of the 1970s, when writers as well as artists were seeking new audiences, Olsen saw creativity as an enormous and universal capacity that could nonetheless be extinguished by a whole range of social conditions. For most women the social conditions that kept them from reaching an audience were crushing—poverty, race, cultural expectations, institutional barriers.[1]

In the last chapter, I discussed how some women found a place for their creative work in the marketplace. In this section I examine the formation of audiences. This is difficult because American historians have not considered audiences in any systematic way. Analyzing who views art, even without considering much about what they take away from that viewing, leads us into some convoluted byways of history. I move now from the modern era, when Anglo artists confidently felt they could find or create a few large themes to describe America or Americans, into a postmodern world in which many competing themes appear.[2]

In this chapter I examine the hungry eye: the woman searching for her own creative past, her own center; the man searching for an understanding of his own experience through those of women. I explore several stories to see where they lead us. The first story is about the audiences for Pomo baskets, the second about the audience for dance, and the third about the audiences created by the feminist art movement of southern California. Postmodernism, I believe, can help us by holding many narratives and many cultures, by allowing us to learn from competing and multicultural themes. This, then, is my search for audiences.

First, let's look back at northern California in the 1950s when Pomo women were still making baskets but not selling them on the market. Annie Burke, a fine Pomo basketmaker, was worried that she was one of the last of the basketmakers. By withdrawing from the marketplace, basketmakers had maintained their art, but they had narrowed their audience and reduced production of baskets to a small number. Burke's concern had grown during the prior decade, and in the 1940s she began to show her baskets at local fairs. She noticed what a positive response people had to her baskets. As she watched the audience admire her art, she decided that the art should be preserved. Burke instructed her daughter that when she died, her baskets were not to be destroyed according to tradition. Instead, they should be preserved and displayed.

Annie Burke had made a trip to the Smithsonian and found the Pomo baskets, collected so assiduously years before, entombed and forgotten. When Burke died in 1962, her daughter, Elsie Allen, was sixty-two years old. As a child she had learned to make baskets from Annie, but had little time to devote to the art and had made only a few in the 1920s and 1930s. She decided to commit the remainder of her life to her mother's wish that the baskets have an audience. Elsie preserved her mother's baskets and began making more of her own. Between 1969 and 1971 Elsie finished fifty-four baskets and gave lessons to whomever she could reach. In February 1973 there was a knock on the door. When she opened it, a young woman stood there. The young woman introduced herself as a niece, Susan Billy.[3]

Susan later told the story this way. She was born in South Dakota in 1951. Her father was Pomo, but he had taken a job in South Dakota and then one in Richmond, Virginia. "My father had some of my grandmother's baskets; his mother's baskets. All the time I was growing up, they were very revered in our home. It seemed like in all our homes, we had these built-in shelves in the living room and the baskets were kept there.... I was real fascinated by them, all the time, growing-up. I would always ask my father, 'How did they make these baskets? Where did it start? How does the color end? How does it change?' I just couldn't figure it out! And I would look at those baskets for a long time... and he always told me I could one day go look up my Aunt Elsie and knock on her door and she could tell me the answers to these questions I had. ... [I had] this fascination with these baskets. I never could really put it out of my mind. It was just part of me from all the time I grew up and was around these baskets. I felt like I was working toward it but I had to do all these other things.... I traveled, lived a bunch of different places. ... But in the back of my mind ... was these baskets, and this Aunt Elsie ... and that I was going to find out my answers!"[4]

By November 1973 Susan was working in a vegetarian restaurant in the Bay Area. Fed up with her job, she quit. She continued her story:

I called my uncle the next morning and I told him I wanted to move into my grandmother's house. He said, "Why do you want to do that? Nobody wants to live there.... No one's lived there since your grandmother passed away." I said, "Well, I want to live there. I have this Auntie I have to go look up. I've got some questions that I need to talk to her about...." By February, I was ready. It was a Wednesday. I remember I went up to her house and I knocked on the door. I'd hitchhiked—I didn't have a car. I hitchhiked up from Hopland and I knocked on her door. I said, "You know, you don't know me but I'm your relative.... I'm Susan Billy. All my life, my daddy told me that you could answer some questions for me about the baskets. I would like to learn how to make the baskets. I'd like to learn about them."

Elsie told her to come back the next day when she would be giving a class in Ukiah. "As I walked across the threshold of the door," Susan said, "she looked up and held her hand out.... She had an awl in her hand, the one she'd been using. She said, 'This is for you.' I kind of looked at it. She said, 'It was your grandmother's. It was passed on to me when she passed away.' She said, 'Last night after you left, I got to thinking that I'd only been given this for safekeeping. It's really for you.' She handed me my grandmother's knife and her awl,... a bundle of white roots, and black roots and willows—things that I needed. I started that day: my work with the baskets and with Elsie."[5]

What did Susan's story have to do with twentieth-century audiences for western women's art? That was what I wanted to know. Lawrence Levine has a theory about what happened to culture at the turn of the twentieth century. He says that as the postfrontier culture took form, a transformation in that culture occurred, a reordering, a placing of certain types of culture in a privileged position. Levine calls it the "sacralization of culture," the separation of the audience into popular and elite, with separate spaces for each type of culture and performer. The new culture elevated a few artists as heroic geniuses and devalued the production of art by many individuals. Photography, according to these criteria, was too accessible and reproduced too many details to be considered real art except when reinterpreted and modeled on painting. Artists gained control over audiences, who became merely spectators rather than participants in creating culture. Levine terms this the "taming of the audience."[6]

In the new cultural hierarchy, Europe became the arbiter of eastern American taste, the East of western taste, and everywhere the city dominated the hinterland. The East became a consumer of things western—material objects, landscape, exploits. The Goetzmanns called this hunger for things western "The West of the Imagination."[7]

In the West, San Francisco occupied a special place in the cultural hierarchy since the early nineteenth century. San Francisco continued to act as a mediator of things western, imitating the East most actively in its creation of new cultural institutions, building museums, symphonies, public libraries, and art institutes. Through these trappings of high culture, San Francisco maintained its role as the cultural capital of the West, creating its own variation of the new culture. So far so good, but where do gender and ethnicity, the ordering of culture by sex and cultural differences fit in? What happened to women, particularly to ethnic women, during this transformation?

Levine's theory tells us nothing about how gender and ethnicity function in relation to audiences. The Anglo-American audience for Pomo baskets might have persisted through this turn-of-the-century transition, but neither collectors nor tourists had access to these particular Indian baskets. The baskets were available either to a Pomo audience, for which they had a special cultural significance, or to anthropologists who might venture into museums to do "scientific" research on basketry. A small audience interested in Indian art as an American antiquity kept interest alive in Indian baskets, but—except in New Mexico—they did little to reinterest Indian peoples in their own traditional arts.

Thus Allen performed a special function, transmitting basketmaking techniques, especially to Pomo, but to others as well, and explaining the art of basketmaking and the aesthetic appreciation of fine baskets again to Pomo and to a larger group of Anglo-Americans. Through Allen's efforts, a disappearing tradition of women's art was revitalized. Allen acted as a mediator between the art object and audience.

Similar changes seemed to be taking place in the audiences for other traditional Indian women's art in the 1960s. Beading and pottery, along with basketry, underwent revival and expansion as audiences increasingly wished to look and to buy. As audiences developed, so too did an art industry that distributed this art.[8]

Can we move from generalizations about an audience for one art, or even different arts by different Indian peoples, to a cross-cultural look at artistic creation? What would happen if we looked at the performing arts, for example dance?

Indian dances retained an essentially separate place in the performing arts. Anglos regarded them as separate, exotic dances, to be suppressed when necessary for public policy, to be watched as exotic entertainment by tourist audiences, and to be viewed by a specially trained elite group of scholar spectators who could explain to Anglos the significance of the dance as they did other aspects of Indian life. During the 1870s and 1890s dance-based religious revivals called "Ghost Dances" spread among western Indian tribes as a way to preserve their cultures and to resist white dominance and population declines. Many of the 1870 dances were openly antiwhite. In response the United States suppressed many Indian dances. Between 1873 and 1912, for example, the Mescalero Apache of New Mexico could not publicly perform their community dances for young women coming of age. The government considered these and similar dances as forms of cultural resistance. Therefore, it allowed Indian dances to be performed in public only in certain places and at certain times, among them Wild West shows, fairs, and at the Indian pueblos of New Mexico.[9]

Early Anglo visitors were shocked at the sexual explicitness of Pueblo dances and the lack of embarrassment of Mexican women who viewed them. Many Pueblos gradually sanitized their public dances, modifying or eliminating sexual imagery until it was deemed acceptable for a new audience that included Anglo women. As late as the 1920s the Commissioner of Indian Affairs attempted to suppress Pueblo dances, this time with the argument that they interfered with a sense of time management.[10]

Most of the dances that continued to be presented for the public seem to have featured men. The wild west show became the setting in which most postfrontier era audiences watched Indian dances. There, Sioux men showed their artistry, especially in the Ghost Dance. In the 1920s increasing numbers of Anglos visited Pueblo villages to observe dances. There, Native American women provided an audience for male dances and participated in women's community dances.[11]

Among the Kashaya Pomo, women began to take primary responsibility for community dances in the 1920s. Most females had been excluded as either participants or observers of traditional male rituals, though they had participated in community dances. As dances assumed a role of cultural survival in the Ghost Dances of the 1870s, more women joined in. With the Bole-maru, a dance based on inspiration from dreams and sequences from old dance cycles, they began to participate in even greater numbers. Thereafter, women began to announce revelations and to encourage the maintenance of the secular dances. The *maru*, the person who called the dance, was not herself a participant. In the Bole-maru women wore specially decorated calico dresses and held brightly colored scarves or bandannas in their hands. Later, all-female dances were held. In the 1950s Essie Parrish, a Kashaya Pomo, led women in dances that combined traditional Pomo and Christian elements. She sang of the power of women and allowed anthropologists to film the ceremony.[12]

The disappearance of Pomo males from the dance may have been a measure of their assimilation into the dominant Euro-American male culture where males seldom danced before audiences in the late nineteenth and early twentieth centuries. In the American West women had always danced for men—sometimes in eroticized dance, but also in a variety of European ethnic dances, Irish clogs, German schottisches, and Spanish fandangos. Skilled women emerged to entertain a diverse audience in popular concert halls. Lotta Crabtree first made her reputation with male audiences in western mining towns. By 1880 she had formed her own company to tour the West and South, and by the turn of the century she was the richest performer in America. She was popular with audiences in the East as well as in Europe and was representative of the dancer who played to mixed gender and class audiences of the nineteenth century.[13]

The rich dance culture out of which Crabtree emerged, continued to provide postfrontier audiences with entertainment. San Francisco dance culture, both participatory and exhibitionary, remained fluid and complex during the postfrontier era. The San Francisco stage hosted circuses, gymnasts, minstrels, skirt dancers, Kanaka women dancing the Hula, blacks performing plantation dances, black comedians, pantomime, Spanish dances. Dancing for the public and dancing with the public provided fortunes for a few and a comfortable living for many women. As this culture fragmented, two separate audiences developed for women dancers. One was a primarily male audience before which they could perform erotic dancing. The other was a mixed middle-class and often ethnically segregated audience before which they had to develop a different type of dancing.[14]

The growing separation was clearest in Isadora Duncan's career. Duncan grew up participating in the complex popular dance culture of northern California, where Indian, Spanish, Mexican, and European dances mingled. She began her dance career performing on the stage, touring small towns up and down California. Like other dancers of the time, she began to seek a more specialized audience, to transform her dances into stage productions for a middle-class and female audience.[15]

In the first decade of the twentieth century, Duncan was not alone in looking for a new style and a new audience. Anglo women studied the dances of other cultures; distilled a type of classical, or ideal, dance; then presented it in sanitized versions to audiences that included increasing numbers of middle-class Anglo women. Duncan competed with a number of other women who emerged from the California dance culture to capture audiences and provide models.

Maud Allan was one competitor. She was born in Toronto but grew up in San Francisco and studied music in Berlin, began to interpret music impressionistically and to dance barefoot, as did Duncan in the early years of the century. A letter from Maud's mother in 1904 revealed her concern about the audiences for whom Maud danced. Allan had a Salome dance in which she wrapped her body in veils. In Europe she could do her dance before elite audiences, but in California the audience for concert dance was not yet established. Mama's letter indicated that the family was concerned that Allan might have to sing in the ten-cent shows and free-beer dives where dancers depended on tips and a percentage of the price of beer they sold in the early hours of the morning. A friend advised Allan to stay in Europe and "not take any chances with the dance over here." Mama advised Maud to "give up trying to come before the public," to come home and take what the family could provide. "What is the use of it after all?" asked Mama.[16]

Allan did not return to the United States until 1910, when she made her American debut in Boston with an ensemble from the Boston Symphony. Art dance was by then established, with an elite audience. Duncan had returned in 1908 and appeared at the Metropolitan Opera House with the New York Symphony. In 1911, when Ruth St.

Denis performed at the Mason Opera House in Los Angeles, her concert was respectable enough for the Santa Barbara physician Dr. George
Graham to take his daughter, Martha. In 1916, two years after Dr. Graham died, Martha's mother allowed her to enroll at the Ruth St. Denis
School of Dancing and Related Arts.[17]

The beer hall audiences never disappeared in San Francisco, but
middle-class women attempted to curtail the performances of working-
class women in them. In the second decade of the twentieth century,
San Francisco's middle-class women's clubs helped suppress Barbary
Coast dancing in the halls that Mama had warned Maud Allan about.
Dance halls provided places where working-class women could participate and perform, being paid to dance with customers. Club members,
claiming that dance halls took advantage of women, eventually closed
down the halls, turning male participants into spectators and women
into performers only. Strip joints provided male customers with scantily clad females to watch and places where white, working-class women
exposed their bodies as a primary function of their art, however skilled.
Middle-class women found their audiences in the concert hall and the
dance style that came to be called modern dance. African American
and Mexican American women continued to dance, but usually not
before assembled middle-class audiences.[18]

Those Mexican American women who danced during this period
drew from a different tradition. Mexican women had early successes in
dance. Lola Montez was wildly popular with audiences. In the 1890s a
number of Mexican women—Cachuchak Matildaita, Corinne, Papinta,
Lola Y berri, La Gardenia, La Estrellita, La Belle Guerrero—all performed in San Francisco. All were billed as "Spanish dancers" although
some were from Spain, some from Mexico, and some native-born Americans. Papinta was born in San Francisco, began dancing in public at
the Chicago World's Fair in 1893, and was still dancing in 1900.[19]

Few of these dancers gained national prominence after the turn of
the century as did Anglo-American dancers. Most found their audiences along the Mexican border where women danced in *carpas*, the
circus tents that brought plays, interspersed with songs, skits, and dances
to Mexican Americans and Mexican immigrants. These dancers often
performed as part of family troupes. After the 1920s American burlesque companies began to move into urban Hispanic theaters providing scantily clad chorus lines of "bellisimas." Dolores Del Rio, the Mexi-

can born actress, did not dance publicly before arriving in Hollywood in the early 1920s. Her success in films brought star-struck Hispanos to Hollywood hoping for similar fame, but she left no dance legacy for young women struggling through vaudevillian routines in the *carpas*. They brought enjoyment to many, but none achieved the success of singer Lydia Mendoza who began to find an audience among the rural border working class in the 1930s.[20]

It seems unlikely that most western women of color could have made the transition from the enormously popular vaudevillian dance tradition to elite concert dance in the first two decades of the twentieth century. Women of enormous talent, such as African American Josephine Baker, found the United States inhospitable in the 1920s, though scantily clad black dancers were welcomed by white audiences at the Cotton Club in Harlem and black women participated in a vigorous participatory dance culture in western communities. The prejudice against black concert dance lingered on into the 1930s keeping dancers like Katherine Dunham, who wished to incorporate some elements of African dance with American popular dance for the stage, from gaining the success and acclaim they deserved. Women of color who wished to dance found the elite performing arts establishment firmly closed to them. Their dance remained participatory and uncommercialized. They were their own audience.[21]

Anglo-Americans seemed to fear that black ethnic dance, with its emphasis on pelvic movement, would encourage uncontrolled sexuality in white audiences. Such fear of sexuality led Duncan to exclude jazz dance from her vision of America dancing. For her, African American dance movement could not be representative of Americans. Only movement of the upper body, a body liberated from the rigidity of ballet but nonetheless held under strict control, could be truly American. The solar plexus, not the pelvis was the basis of dance for Duncan. For American dance to be truly inclusive, of course, it had to come from all parts of the body and all cultural traditions.[22]

Western Anglo women, then, became the exemplars of modern concert dance. Like other forms of modern art, modern dance developed in the 1920s and 1930s into an art form stressing the ideal rather than the local, the solo artist rather than the ensemble, an overreaching theme with little detail, and little audience participation. As one critic has noted, Allan, Duncan, and St. Denis liberated dance from the stereotype of the old ballet, but they also liberated dance from the old audiences. Martha Graham placed dance on the level of other modern arts in the United States, but as a preeminently female art form (she did not include men in her dance troupe for many years) and for a predominantly female audience. She exposed the female form encased in a modern shell, much as modern style in architecture encased and covered the skeleton of modern buildings. Graham studied American Indian and African dance, but they were all subsumed in the abstract dance. That dance was often a stylized resolution of the inner conflicts that Anglo women were expected to have.[23]

Modern dance did not replace ballet, the dance that rigidly controlled women's bodies. Nor did it replace the popular dance that still found a place on the stage stylized in musical comedy. And it competed directly with the growing popularity of jazz dance. In 1927 Duncan envisioned an ideal American dance performed in a style that drew from the European tradition, incorporated Indian dance, and emphasized movement of the upper body. Jazz dance had overtaken the dancing public, which participated in it eagerly during the 1920s, and despite the control that modern dance asserted on the stage, Duncan feared that Americans might make jazz their national dance. Jazz was a countertext of this era when modern dance, created by western Anglo women, reached its ascendancy in the East.[24]

Modern dance was still part of the vanguard arts in the 1930s. Graham refused to commercialize her art; thus, her audiences remained relatively small. Agnes de Mille, another western dancer, finally merged ballet, modern, and western folk dance with the popular musical form and a more traditional context to reach the widest audiences.

The result was *Rodeo*. The plot was similar to those that playwright Zoë Akins was so successfully exploring in modern drama, a strong woman assuming a feminine role to attract a man: in this case a western cowgirl who, in de Mille's words, "dressed and acted as a man," then put on a skirt and got her man. The ballet troupe worked its way eastward across the United States in the summer of 1942 and opened in New York on October 16. de Mille, who danced the lead, took twenty-two curtain calls holding a bunch of American corn tied with red, white, and blue ribbons. The fiddlers beat their bows on their instruments, the other musicians yelled. With *Rodeo*, de Mille brought East and West together, birthed a new style, and found a new audience.[25]

The most successful merging of western themes and style for de Mille came with the production of *Oklahoma!* in 1944. In some ways *Oklahoma!* symbolized the apex of the modern popular audience. The musical ran for more than five years in New York City and for nine and a half years as a road show, closing in 1954. It ran three and a half years in London and for years more in the British provinces. An estimated fifty-five million people saw it; another eight hundred thousand bought records of the soundtrack. In 1955 the film brought millions to the theater.[26]

Oklahoma! had mobilized a vast audience. Its peak period of popularity, from 1944 to 1955, coincided with the last flourishing of modernism and New York's ascendancy to a new domination of art. During this post–World War II period Anglo males increased their profits and control over the merchandising of culture and admitted only a few women, such as Graham and de Mille, to their pantheon. The rapid mobilization of a popular audience under the banner of late modernism brought the final downfall of its long rise to popularity. What had once been the property of an elite vanguard of artists, and small groups of concessionaires, was now controlled by a relatively small group that packaged elite culture for the masses. While white middle-class women were being mobilized in increasing numbers as audiences for the postwar culture, they were able to affect the content and context of that culture less and less. When the new counterculture took form in the beat movement, Anglo women again found themselves frozen out.

New York dominated the visual as well as the performing arts in the 1950s, and male artists occupied center stage. They were also, rather surprisingly, western. Several of the most famous abstract expressionists, including Jackson Pollock, Mark Rothko, Robert Motherwell, and Clyfford Still, had spent all or part of their youth in the West. Pollock became the exemplar of the intuitive artist absorbed with the expression of his own personality. Some historians have even argued that abstract expressionism, that quintessence of late-modern style, was an art of the American West. Pollock and abstract expressionism, ridiculed by *Life* magazine in 1949, were soon the toast of the town. Like Agnes de Mille, Pollock represented symbolically the vitality of western Anglo civilization to postwar America. These young white men, said the critics, painted from "inner impulse without an ear to what the critic or spectator may feel [with] exuberance, independence, native sensibility." In fact, their art was highly commercialized and carefully packaged for the new consumer of visual arts. The wealthy became direct consumers of this art through an increasing number of galleries. The middle class viewed it in an expanding number of modern art museums, many designed in the international style.[27]

Those galleries and museums expanded in the hinterland as well. The Bay Area, especially, became a regional center for the new modern art. But regional centers were little duplicates of New York. Audiences in San Francisco saw what audiences in New York saw. Museums and patrons bought the same kind of art. Audiences came in increasing numbers as the affluence of the middle class increased in the 1960s, but they came to an art that neither reflected their lives nor their values. Audiences were trained in increasing numbers in colleges to appreciate modern art, especially modern New York art, as the culmination of European civilization. But that civilization had become a white male vision. And white males spoke mainly to each other, inviting others to listen.[28]

What happened to western Anglo women artists during the rise of abstract expressionism to a place of dominance in the postwar world? Women had helped form audiences for modern art in the West during the 1920s. They had opened private galleries to show contemporary art, introduced German expressionism to Bay Area audiences, directed museums that adventurously exhibited modern art. Women artists participated in government-sponsored public projects, especially the mural movement in California in the 1930s. Women artists had felt themselves to be an essential part of the visual arts culture of the 1930s.[29]

After World War II that visual arts culture changed. The government no longer had a publicly sponsored arts program. Instead it offered subsidies to veterans, many of whom chose to study art. In time those artists absorbed attitudes that reached public audiences. Hassel Smith, who began teaching at the California School of Fine Arts (CSFA) in 1945, welcomed the change from female to male students. Before, he said, the place was "just crawling with socialites. The G.I. Bill brought in... a very swinging bunch [of] working artists." Generally male teachers predominated and they saw men as the main audience, an audience that had to be taught how to see and create art. By 1950, when this first group of men had been initiated, CSFA director Douglas MacAgy recalled: "I was concerned about an impending change in the quality of the student body [because the] postwar pool of mature students was dwindling" and would be replaced by "throngs of girls who can't make college and want to mark time while they look for husbands." MacAgy resigned too soon, for the Korean War brought a new batch of returning veterans. When Joan Beaty (later Brown) arrived at CSFA in 1955 as a student, she found about two hundred students. Only a few were women; scores were veterans, most of them wearing sandals and playing bongo drums. She went right out and bought herself some sandals.[30]

Like many women artists of this generation, Joan Brown survived through close relationships with male artists and by enduring the increasing isolation from the most prestigious students and public audiences of the 1960s. Administrators at CSFA consistently shunted Brown to low-paying night classes; she found new audiences teaching children and the handicapped. Brown later commented: "It was tough at that time, but I would never have had the experience of working with all those different groups of people if I had been able to sail from school into—like many of my male peers did—a university or college job."[31]

At the top a male elite consolidated its control during the 1960s. Women were a majority of the art students at the undergraduate and graduate level, but white males managed to keep the most prestigious teaching jobs for themselves, increased their percentage of the faculties, and dominated galleries and museums. Many women found individual male artists easy to work with, but the institutional sexism and racism increased as the cultural structures of the 1950s and 1960s became more enmeshed in economics and politics. Critics acted increasingly as gatekeepers, as judges for juried shows and museum exhibits. As a whole, critics (including a few Anglo women) discouraged audiences from taking the work of women artists seriously, trivialized their work as lacking scope and energy, and emphasized their femaleness rather than their creativity. Art history became a province inhabited almost exclusively by Anglo male artists, even when taught by women. As art became big business and universities burgeoned to teach the masses who came through the academic doors, white women and all people of color found themselves increasingly marginalized in a system that had in the 1930s seemed to be more open and democratic.

Some of America's most noted women artists were from California and did receive recognition during this period. Lithographer June

Wayne, sculptor Claire Falkenstein, painter Helen Lundebert, potters Joyce Treiman and Beatrice Wood were among the best-known Anglo artists. Many of these women had participated in the WPA projects of the 1930s, where they had been taken seriously as artists and had made their way by being determined and creative. A few younger artists, such as Joan Brown, survived by helping men organize galleries and manage critics, and through their sheer determination to be in the vanguard. New York art dealer George Staempfli put Brown on a stipend in return for the exclusive right to sell her work in the late 1950s. As a result, she was the youngest artist in the "Young America 1960" show at the Whitney Museum in New York.[32]

Women of color who had no access to white audiences found their own separate audiences in the 1960s. California-born Ruth Azawa, who grew up on a farm in southern California, received her first art lessons from Japanese-American artists while interned during World War II. With the help of Quakers she received a scholarship to Black Mountain College, where she studied with Josef Albers. When she moved to the Bay Area, Azawa worked at home, outside the establishment, with her husband's support. African American Betty Saar, born in Pasadena, found her support in a black community and a black culture that she adapted to the popular southern California tradition of assemblage (the incorporation of found objects into paintings). Other black women lent their support to documenting the lives and work of black visual, performing, and literary artists. Camille Billop, along with her husband, developed the Hatch-Billops Collection of African American art. Samella Lewis, who came to Los Angeles in 1969, set up a gallery to exhibit the work of black artists, founded the Museum of African American Art and the quarterly *Black Art*, and edited books on the history of African American art.[33]

Anglo women artists in southern California increasingly found they faced similar exclusion from access to audiences. Women were being admitted to art schools in large numbers by the early 1960s—more than 50 percent of undergraduate and graduate art majors in California were women—but the percentage of women on art faculties steadily declined, from 22 percent in 1963 to 19 percent in 1974. Samella Lewis, who later became professor of art history at Scripps College, pointed out another problem. Although large numbers of women were being trained and were practicing their art, no one was explaining the art of women and people of color. Art historians never talked about their art; therefore, critics, who interpreted for audiences, did not know how to evaluate it. If art validated people, as Lewis believed, then these artists and people like them were not being validated through the mainstream art structure.[34]

That certainly seemed to be true. Between 1961 and 1971 the prestigious Los Angeles County Museum gave one-artist shows to fifty-two males but only one female, a photographer. The group shows exhibited 684 men and 29 women. Among California museums only the Oakland Museum of Art made a place for relatively large numbers of women artists. Women artists did best in competitive juried shows where the identity of the artists was unknown and thus artists could not be judged by sex. In these shows, women's art appeared in proportion to the number who entered. When women did manage to get shows, reviewers often ignored them, or if they did not, frequently used sexist stereotypes that assigned feminine adjectives as pejoratives.[35]

The exhibit that finally spurred women to action was called "Art and Technology." This 1968 exhibit in Los Angeles did not include a single woman artist. Enraged women organized protest meetings and formed the Los Angeles Council of Women Artists (LACWA). The council documented discrimination in exhibits and asked women to testify about their experiences before a special public hearing of the California Commission on the Status of Women. Organizers appealed to older women who had established their reputations during the more open periods of the 1930s and 1940s and who had managed to survive the 1950s. Lithographer June Wayne was one of them.[36]

June Wayne summed up the situation in an article reprinted in the report. Wayne estimated three hundred artists for every gallery spot. The answer, she argued, was not to reduce the pool of artists but to develop the market system to reach a broader audience. "The future of the art world in this country," she wrote, "will be profoundly influenced by the self-reevaluation of women and minority artists who are reversing a previously passive acceptance of outside pressures." She saw artists opening studios to the public, establishing artist-owned cooperative corporations, forming guilds that could obtain equitable tax reforms, opening up the news media to culture, providing art news from trained art reporters, and representing artists on policy-making boards of museums. Self-determination, she argued, could lead to a large national role for creative people of every kind to perform "those life enhancement services that revaluation of the quality of life suggests is necessary to the survival of the species."[37]

This was a vast reconceptualization of the role of the artist, the market, and the audience. It emerged from the first years of the women's movement in southern California. But this group was not alone in the late 1960s, nor were all of the ideas generated by its members. A number of notions were distilled from a wide range of suggestions. Nevertheless, the particular confluence of art and politics in southern California allowed women such as June Wayne to see the needs and possibilities for the formation of a new art world that would welcome and find space for Anglo women and people of color, that would be reorganized to give artists more direct access to audiences. In southern California women artists saw their work as part of an experiment that might lead to such a new possibility.

The acceptance of women's experience and history as a suitable realm for visual arts was an event that both released and absorbed an immense amount of energy in southern California. That energy could not be contained within the impulse to reform institutions. It spilled over into a women's movement to create a space of their own where new audiences could be assembled. Eventually the movement for a separate women's space included special courses on women's art; a women's art magazine *Crysalis*; Womanhouse in Los Angeles; the Los Angeles Woman's Building, with a Feminist Studio Workshop; a woman's co-op gallery called double x; a book, *By Our Own Hands*, documenting the artistic tradition of southern California women; and the mammoth art project *The Dinner Party*.[38]

This second phase of the southern California women's art movement drew much of its strength from the anarchistic tendencies that were developing within the California political scene. All over California politically active young people were abandoning their efforts to reform major social institutions and striking out on their own to create alternatives. For women artists this anarchistic phase involved leaving educational institutions and other establishments within which they had so recently achieved a modest place for themselves. Women had managed to move into art teaching positions, at least marginally, in such places as California state universities and in the newly formed California Institute for the Arts (called Cal Arts for short). During the second phase of the women's art movement, they poured into Los Angeles to participate in creating alternative institutions for new audiences, particularly women.

The career of Judy Chicago illustrates both of these stages. Born in 1939, Judy Gerowitz grew up in Chicago, but chose to study art at the University of California at Los Angeles in the 1960s and changed her name to Chicago in 1970 to symbolize her emerging feminism. That year Chicago accepted a position at California State University at Fresno in the San Joaquin Valley, where she started the first Feminist Art Program. The idea of the Feminist Art Program was to experiment with a feminist education for women art students. Fifteen women enrolled in the first program, most of them neither feminists nor formally trained artists. The program attracted women interested in a wide range of visual and performing arts. The group met in a room furnished only with bright carpet scraps and big pillows. Chicago began the class with yoga and stretches, encouraged the women to hug and touch each other, to role play and release their emotions. Once a week, a revolving committee cooked a communal dinner where there was storytelling, family fights, and raucous jokes. The principles of feminist education that evolved from the program were consciousness raising, building a female context and environment (they rented an old barracks building to control the space entirely), female role models (historical figures and guest artists), and permission to make art out of their own experiences as women and find a common female art tradition.[39]

This was a startling new concept. Most modernist artists saw themselves as creating an art that reflected universals. The feminist art movement rejected the concept of individuals expressing the experience of all people. It urged women to translate personal, idiosyncratic visions into the visual arts and to seek a female tradition in art. It admonished them to see women's art traditions not as bizarre exceptions to formal art nor as trivial, personal, domestic art, but as a central theme in art. Rejecting the single vision of modernism that excluded or marginalized the cultures of Anglo women and people of color, the women's art movement substituted a pluralistic vision of society. As a part of this new emphasis, women could now experiment with a broad realm of cultures and approaches. And experiment they did, with icons, with the psychological self, the self and the body and sexuality, the self and the cosmos, the self as child, mother and self, the self in history, and the self in ethnic cultures.[40]

The artists at Fresno translated this experience into a wide range of media, styles, and techniques. They used photography, collage, assemblage, films, performances, videos, narratives, paintings, drawings, writings, environments, and installations. Individual artists had practiced in all of these styles and the assemblage movement was particularly strong in southern California at the time, but Chicago and the Fresno group encouraged students to use all of them in explaining women's experiences as females in a self-consciously feminist way.

Chicago could achieve this outrageously nontraditional program at Fresno State University because at the time she had the support of feminists within the university administration. She was also able to get institutional support from the California Institute of the Arts. The faculty there were experimenting with many nontraditional art forms. The management of the school was enormously tolerant of this whole weird environment, one participant later said. Miriam Schapiro, a successful New York artist whose husband was the new dean at Cal Arts, said she convinced the men to invite Chicago to join the faculty and to let the two women teach a feminist art program together. Chicago was a highly visible publicist for her new teaching techniques and had lectured at a number of California universities, including the University of California at San Diego where she met Schapiro. In the fall of 1972 the new Cal Arts program created Womanhouse, a collaborative environment and showcase for the new feminist art.[41]

The art at Womanhouse revealed the experiences of women; it challenged the relegation of women to the private sphere; and it offered a critique of the way society viewed—and constructed—women's roles and identities. Multimedia and multistyle, Womanhouse art combined autobiography and narrative with women's traditional arts, such as needlework. Womanhouse defined art as a socially critical and participatory activity designed to promote audience dialogue and discussion. It brought feminist art before a vast public audience. All the major national networks and journals discussed it as the first large-scale example of feminist art. The following year women artists opened Womanspace gallery. Eventually Womanspace had more than twelve hundred members, whose exhibits attracted capacity crowds. The movement had found its audience. Artists and audiences now creatively supported one another.[42]

In 1973 Judy Chicago, Sheila de Bretteville, and Arlene Raven resigned from their teaching jobs at Cal Arts. Together with Womanspace gallery and other feminist organizations, they founded the Los Angeles Woman's Building, with its Feminist Studio Workshop (FSW). At the center of the FSW curriculum was the question of audiences, specifically, what process one used to build a community that included a wider audience. The 1970s saw an opening up of art to the public and a blurring of the rigid categories into which the art establishment had placed artists of different styles and forms—and their audiences. The Woman's Building, the FSW (which eventually graduated over three hundred artists and graphics designers), the nonprofit gallery double x, the women's cultural arts magazine *Crysalis* (with its thirteen thousand subscribers), and *The Dinner Party* presented the new feminist art to audiences.[43]

The Dinner Party began as a giant visual history of women. Over a period of five years, four hundred artists and craftspeople helped Chicago design and execute *The Dinner Party* in painted porcelain and needlework. *The Dinner Party* was an equilateral triangular table forty-eight feet on each side set with thirty-nine places, each representing a historic or legendary woman. The artists used china painting and needlework, two traditional women's arts, but employed female sexual symbolism, what Chicago called "butterfly vagina plates". The table rested on a floor inscribed with the names of 999 historic women.

The Dinner Party opened in July 1979 to record crowds at San Francisco's Museum of Modern Art. It then moved to Chicago where it also proved to be immensely popular. Before it arrived in Rochester, New York, the show was cancelled. Apparently, a controversy arose over the use of money raised for the show, for consciousness raising about sexism in society and the art world. Despite cancellation in Rochester and several other eastern cities, *The Dinner Party* toured six countries during the next decade; more than a million people saw it. Gradually the traditional art establishments opened their doors to women artists.[44]

The feminist cultural movement of the 1970s gave women permission to evoke their own experiences as women and as members of different cultures in a wide variety of creative forms. It also urged them to present those experiences publicly to new audiences. Most people in the first phase of this cultural revolution saw themselves in opposition to the central modernist tradition. And they did not realize how quickly the center would disintegrate once their energies were directed against it. As postmodernism began to take shape, political problems arose that affected the cultural revolution. The old liberal political center dissolved and was replaced by political groups of the right. The feminism created by the cultural movement of the 1970s now had to come to terms with a postmodern movement that at times seemed capable of rendering women invisible once more.

Opening the doors of traditional art worlds to women in Los Angeles also lessened the need for a central alternative space. New York never had a single center like the Woman's Building, in part because the art scene there was so large and diverse. By the 1980s, the Los Angeles art market had grown almost as large, powerful, and diverse as that in New York. The building closed in 1991.[45]

By 1991 feminism had changed as well. Some Anglo-American artists had thought they must speak in one voice for all women. Yet the disintegration of modernism, in which they had participated so actively, introduced many ways to see and express the relationship of women to the old dominant culture and to the many new cultures struggling for public audiences. Feminism gave rise to feminisms. Women found they did not have to, nor could they, speak in one voice to an audience so vast and various. Women in cultures of different regions, classes, and ethnicities had to speak in many voices.

These voices also had to be capable of speaking to audiences of the many ways in which women had been subordinated. Part of the postmodern cultural critique also came from women reacting to the colonialism imposed by Europeans and Americans in other countries and in their own. Women from formerly colonized peoples remained skeptical that women within "Western civilizations" could understand civilizations that had been politically subordinated by them. To create an image of a multicultural America meant not only to value cultures of women as well as men, but also to cross boundaries and borders. It meant, art critic Lucy Lippard maintained, searching for cultures in the eddies that provided sanctuaries outside the mainstream at home, and to the South American, African, and Asian cultures that fed these countercurrents.[46]

That is what Susan Billy had to do with audiences. The Pomo people, in nourishing their cultural tradition of basketmaking and preserving it, enabled her to return to it and to cultural nourishment. When the Pomo women wove baskets, they left a dau, a path for Quail Woman to return and inspect their creative work. Making cultural creations accessible to people allows them to inspect, to affirm, to nourish, and to be nourished. Not to have an audience, and not to be an audience, as Olsen said, is a kind of death.

Art that nourishes the self and community has been an essential part of art in the American West. Pomo women judged and ranked artists within their communities. The community knew who produced the best art. Some of that art became commodified as artists struggled to survive. Yet it was the connection between the artist and the community that gave life and vitality to the art. And the community expected that the artist would return a part of what she earned through the sale of that art to the community.

Duncan had a vision of America dancing, but she could not quite bring herself to let everyone join in the dance. Her vision excluded some of the most creative dance traditions in America. In western America there would be many artists and many audiences. The body moving in space could not be contained within a tradition that excluded dances that nourished so many peoples. Commercialization of dance as a performing art could provide income for some and mobilize audiences, but highly commercialized and controlled dance could not provide nourishment for all the artists and audiences that regional, cultural, and participatory dance provided.

The feminist art movement of southern California tried to provide an opening for participatory art, bringing new visions to new audiences. Like dance, it threatened to open new ways of looking at and experiencing the body and so challenged mainstream elite audiences and the establishments of the art world that catered to their needs. Yet southern Californians, who provided openness for the efforts of artists to mobilize new audiences, soon were remobilized by the art world itself toward commodified art. Southern California, which nourished creativity in the 1970s, turned to nurturing more structured art worlds in the 1980s. Women lost most of the audiences they had created, in part because they lacked the resources and energy their mobilization had required. Like other community art cultures energized by the cultural critique of the 1970s, it proved difficult to sustain the art culture constructed by feminism.

In the western borderlands, women redefined American culture and searched for audiences with whom to collaborate in that redefinition. To continue that process, to join together many cultures, to see Duncan's dancing America as truly multicultural will take new audiences that help women create, help them maintain lives that allow the space and energy to create. These audiences will have to recognize, understand, and value many ways of representing that creativity.

PART TWO

5

WITH THESE WORDS
SILENCES/VOICES

"Blessed are those who listen when no one is left to speak," wrote Linda Hogan in the poem "Blessing" published in the 1970s. She was thinking about her family, her Chickasaw family in Oklahoma, when she wrote that poem. "At the time I thought of Indian people as vanishing and that our stories and histories were disappearing," she said. But she came to realize that was not true: "The people will listen to the world and translate it into a human tongue." The process of doing that is especially difficult for women who are not white and middle class. "It's like trying to break in and survive, versus trying to have a position equal to a white man in a corporation," was how Hogan put it. And so it is.[1]

This chapter takes another look at women and creativity. It has to do with a certain select kind of audience—a small group of people who hear, then seek other people who will, in turn, hear them.

What a creative tradition does for women is essentially find people who listen. A select group of people encourage women to speak in various ways. Women who wish to give voice search out these traditions, trying to shape them to their own needs. Those who listen then shape the individual to a cultural tradition they support. Most of the women discussed in this chapter came from poor families. The traditions they found—anthropological, pioneer, and avant-garde (writing experimentally for a small group)—were still taking form in the 1920s and 1930s. To employ those traditions most women had to take time away from work they did in order to survive or after that work had almost exhausted their energies.

These women found their voices because they found listeners. They are western examples of those women Tillie Olsen wrote about in *Silences*. Women's silences and their struggles to write concerned Olsen when she began writing about women's literature in the late 1950s. Coming of age in Omaha, Nebraska, as a second-generation Russian Jew in a family that lived its socialist principles and struggled with working-class poverty gave Olsen a rich experience about which to write. She learned to listen to the people around her. For two years, from 1932 to 1934, she wrote; she also had her first child and moved to San Francisco where she became active in left-wing politics. For the next two decades writing came last, after mothering, political activism, and paid work. Olsen could not write about her experiences. She had no time to be a full-time creative worker with writing as a major concern practiced "habitually, in freed, protected, undistracted time as needed, when it is needed."[2]

Olsen wrote later about the cost of discontinuity and the "weight of things unsaid." Her hands were at other tasks during the years when she should have been writing. After receiving grants in 1956 and 1959 that enabled her to write full-time, she published her first book at age fifty. For the next twenty years Olsen wrote about how women suffered when they could not write, could not give voice to the words they had within. She wrote especially about women who came from working-class families, who struggled to speak. Money, literacy, education, shorter working hours, more humane conditions of life, consciousness—all could allow first-generation writers to speak. But they were still vulnerable to "lessenings and silencing." Long interims between works, fewer books, a kind of marginalization that persisted were their burdens for being born into the working class.[3]

Olsen was one of the first western working-class women who found her way to a new literary tradition in the 1950s. Since the 1950s western women have found an academic literary tradition that has given them support for writing. Through writing classes, grants, and often through jobs, these women found part of what they needed to tell the stories they had heard within their cultures. Many younger women found classrooms where someone first listened to their "voices"; then they found others who urged them to speak. Such places survive precariously today. They did not exist at all for western working-class women in the first half of the twentieth century. The women discussed in this chapter were not the first to struggle to give voice to their stories. But their accounts bear eloquent testimony to the difficulties of shaping a life that will let that voice emerge and finding a tradition through which to express it.[4]

The storytelling tradition was a highly developed skill among western Indian women. During the first decade of the twentieth century, as their children became literate in English and often abandoned parts of their culture, a small number of native women began translating their traditions for outsiders. The search for assistance began just as anthropology was developing as a discipline in the Anglo-American scholarly world. The problem for Indian women, as for others, was to find time—among lives crowded with the tasks of preserving the fabric of families and the texture of cultures—to develop the skills to transmit their knowledge to another culture. In the postfrontier period many native women chose to transmit their information to male recorders. After World War I they had an increasing number of female anthropologists to whom to tell their stories. In the Southwest that collaboration involved Indian women and Anglo anthropologists who were eager to listen to their stories in a new relationship, one sometimes troubled by imperfect communication, but sometimes quite successful in conveying the American Indians' literary tradition.[5]

Some early twentieth-century American Indian women seemed particularly intent on preserving their cultures. A few were eager to tell stories: some because they feared the younger generation would not pass on traditions, others because the elders were no longer able to enforce secrecy. During this time Indians were often more open about their cultures. At Taos, for example, Pueblos became more secretive in the 1920s and 1930s as tourism and the surrounding population increased.[6]

The women told their stories against a backdrop of increasing oppression by Anglo Americans. Indian women were powerful in their own cultures, but their place in Anglo-American society was severely constrained. Many western Indians were subjected to severe social discrimination throughout most of the 1920s and 1930s. In many areas of the West, native peoples were excluded from hospitals, restaurants, and theaters, and not until they organized protests did some of this discrimination end. The voices of Indian women are a powerful reminder that women assumed the role of public as well as domestic conveyors of their cultures.

A number of American Indian women decided to exercise their power through words shared with people outside their culture. Lucy Thompson published a book about her Yurok history in California in 1919. In North Dakota, Maxidiwiac told her story to a son who translated it. Maxidiwiac's story was published in 1921. A Mesquakie woman in Iowa told her life story to Harry and Dalottiwa Lincoln in 1918. Dalottiwa was a Mesquakie-Winnebago who wrote the story phonetically; another Mesquakie paraphrased this version into English; then ethnologist Truman Michelson edited the final version and published it in 1925. Christine Quintasket probably began her autobiography about this time; by 1918 she was teaching, had bought herself a typewriter, and had completed her novel *Cogewea*.[7]

Although the story of Maxidiwiac—better known to her readers as Buffalo Bird Woman—takes us away from the Far West, she was an important part of a new literary tradition. Maxidiwiac's account of Hidatsa agriculture and of her life started me wondering about this question of voice and silence, about transmitting the culture of family, kin, and community to outsiders in order to give it more permanent form. I first read her account nearly twenty years ago, when I was just beginning to write about the lives of rural women. Her work was a model for me in many ways, so it seems appropriate to move to North Dakota to look briefly at her life. The importance for American Indian women of preserving their cultures in new more permanent forms is illustrated in Maxidiwiac's story.

Maxidiwiac was sixty-seven when her only child, Good Bird, brought the ethnographer Gilbert Wilson to her in July of 1906. She spoke no English, but her son explained that Wilson had come to Independence, North Dakota, to study Indian artifacts and how they were made. Maxidiwiac's husband was seventy-six and in frail health. He would die later that fall. She was still robust. Dressed in a ribbon skirt and striped shawl, her dark hair parted neatly in the center and braided, Maxidiwiac stood with her husband and son for a photograph that Wilson snapped in the summer of 1906.[8]

Over the next twelve years Wilson returned each summer to visit with Maxidiwiac and her family. She came to accept his patience and tact as evidence of a sincere desire to document her view of the past. She decided that Wilson could be trusted to tell her life story as she wished it told, to document in words and pictures what she had learned

over a long life. After adopting Wilson in 1909 into her clan of the
Prairie Chicken to ensure his loyalty, Maxidiwiac decided, with Good
Bird as translator and Wilson as transcriber, to tell her story. Once having made that decision, her energy to retell her life seemed endless. "In
the sweltering heat of an August," Wilson wrote, "she has continued
dictation for nine hours, lying down but never flagging in her account
when too weary to sit longer in a chair." Wilson considered her "a born
story teller with a genius for details," with "a quick intelligence and a
memory that is marvelous." In 1910 Wilson wrote, "I have long since
learned not to try to move her when her mind is set." Wilson used her
agricultural descriptions for his dissertation in 1916, published part of
her memoirs in the *St. Paul Farmer* from 1916 to 1917, and in book
form in 1921, as *Waheenee: An Indian Girl's Story*. By 1925 more than
seventy-four thousand copies of her book, *Waheenee*, had sold. Reprinted
in the 1980s, the book has sold thousands more copies.[9]

We know far less about how Yurok author Lucy Thompson actually
wrote her book *To the American Indian*. She began the history of her
people and her life with these words: "I am a pure full-blooded Kla-
math River woman. In our tongue, we call this great river by the name
Health-kick-wer-roy, and I wear the tatoos on my chin that has been
the custom for our women for many generations." Born Che-na-wah
Weitch-ah-wah in 1853, Thompson adopted the name of her Anglo
husband and published under that name in 1916 when she took her
manuscript, unedited, to a print shop in Eureka, California.[10]

As Thompson struggled to translate Yurok language and customs,
she shaped a middle way between traditional and assimilated Yuroks.
Post-contact history had been so painful to the Yuroks that anthropologist Alfred Kroeber once said he could not stand the tears of his
older informants and entirely avoided discussing the recent past.
Thompson tried to come to terms with the two cultures, the old and
the new, and to document the old culture while participating in it,
especially through its dances.[11]

Thompson enlisted the assistance of her family in writing her story.
Husband Milton, a successful Anglo timberman, and daughter Bertha,
a trained nurse, helped her with the book. But the story was emphati-
cally her own: an autobiography of her life and a history of her people.
At one point Thompson wrote, "where my pen has failed to impress,"
and at another referred to one Yurok man as "an unlettered man who

can speak no English." She was proud of her bilingualism, her biculturalism, and her ability to transmit the story of her life and culture to readers of English. Thompson's story, mediated only by her husband and daughter, is told for a general adult readership. She is a literate and proud woman who wrote because she saw the older traditions disappearing; she regarded her narrative as a way to preserve Yurok past and the role of her family in that history. She was autobiographer, historian, and ethnologist, but her book, once published, never moved toward recognition, nor her life toward reputation. The book found its way into libraries and into Yurok ethnology, but not into a broader history of literature, ethnology, or history. Both the book and Thompson remained known only locally. Her silence occurred not because she did not speak, but because there were few to hear—a small audience that cared within a larger culture that did not.[12]

The book by Lucy Thompson is an extraordinary story, told in the American Indian tradition but translated into English. We cannot tell from the book itself what that process of translation and transformation involved in the specific context of Yurok oral traditions or her writing. But Lucy Thompson seemed uniquely successful in compiling her book without the assistance of outside Anglos.

Like Thompson, Christine Quintasket wrote her own books, but she lacked a family who could assist her and relied, instead, on several male literary assistants. The Yakima newspaper man Heister Dean Guie, who helped her edit her Indian stories, suggested eliminating any mention of incest, transvestism, and infanticide. Like Wilson, who published Maxidiwiac's accounts, Guie thought the best popular audience for American Indian stories were children. Another assistant altered her novel before publishing it for her.[13]

Quintasket was born in Idaho in the late 1880s and grew up on her father's ranch near the Colville Reservation in eastern Washington. She grew up as most Salishan children, beginning her training in legends and family history, tales of bravery, and tribal laws at five or six. Her father's grandmother was a famous medicine woman and her mother's mother was noted for her herbal knowledge. Her mother encouraged her to learn the old medicine ways. Because both grandmothers were absent for most of her young life (one dead, the other living in British Columbia), Christine learned storytelling from her adopted grandmother, Teequalt. She learned her love of books from an orphaned white boy, Jimmy Ryan, who lived with her family and worked on the ranch. Jimmy read paperback novels. Christine wrote that when her mother papered the walls of their cabin with the pages of Jimmy's books, "he continued to read from the wall, with me helping to find the next page." Her mother scolded her for being interested in books. She wanted her to learn traditional ways. Quintasket tried to learn both.[14]

During her lifetime Quintasket completed a novel, two collections of stories, and an autobiography. The novel was published in 1927, thirteen years after she completed it, the stories in 1933 and 1976, and the autobiography in 1990. Quintasket was never fully integrated into the anthropological literary tradition. Nor could she find her way to other literary traditions as did later women Indian writers who used university listeners to find their path to broader audiences. Quintasket had to find a literary tradition for a voice already well developed within her culture. Her work touched three traditions: the oral storytelling tradition maintained within Indian cultures, the anthropological tradition being institutionalized and professionalized within the academy, and a written storytelling tradition being reserved more and more for young Anglo-American audiences. Both of the Anglo-American traditions severely restricted what could be translated from the Indian storytelling tradition, especially topics concerning politics and sexuality.

Quintasket began to write in English to preserve the history and culture of the Salishan tribe. Wanting to tell her own story in her own words, she bought a typewriter and lugged it with her around the state of Washington as she worked in the hop fields. "I am trying to write, but lordy with all these mountain pests, I get frantic," she wrote in 1919 while living in a tent. "After working for ten hours in the blazing sun, and cooking my meals, I know I shall not have the time to look over very much mss," she wrote eleven years later to one of the Anglo male collaborators who was helping her publish her novel. Quintasket struggled to find the language and form to transmit her work, as well as the time and energy amid caring for children and working in the hop fields. Her lifelong commitment to the difficult task of writing makes Quintasket, like Maxidiwiac and Thompson, an important model for the creative process I am trying to describe.[15]

In her novel, *Cogewea,* Quintasket moves beyond storytelling to describe the storyteller herself in the person of Stemteema, the grandmother. Stemteema is probably a fictional composite of all the older women who taught the oral tradition, but perhaps especially her adopted grandmother, Teequalt, who supervised Quintasket's spiritual, moral, and traditional training. "She was a great teacher, remembering many of the old ways when out of custom," Quintasket wrote of Teequalt. The fictional Stemteema still wears beaded moccasins and ankle-wraps, a brilliant colored handkerchief bound around her head, ear ornaments, and a plaid shawl. Before telling her stories, Stemteema takes a smoke to put her in the mood to talk and to give her time to gather her thoughts. She smokes kinnikinnick in a stone pipe. Stemteema got the stories from her father and says, "I know they [her forbearers] would want them kept only to their own people if they were here. But they are gone and for me the sunset of the last evening is approaching and I must not carry with me this history.... The story I am telling is true and I want you to keep it after I am gone."[16]

During the 1930s anthropologists would continue to mediate stories, choosing to work with Cheyenne, Arapaho, and Tohono O'odham women. When Maria Chona told her story to anthropologist Ruth Underhill in 1931, she chose a mediator who recognized her strength as a woman and cultural transmitter. Chona was a songmaker and shaman who took pride in her exceptional curing powers and had prestige with her people. The Tohono O'odham faced some of the same problems that other groups had experienced earlier with white communities; perhaps Chona told her story for some of the same reasons other women had—to testify about their lives and their cultures. Another Tohono O'odham shaman, Owl Woman, had sung her songs for Frances Densmore just a few years earlier so that her songs, if not her life story, could also be recorded. Although Underhill emphasized Chona's strength, she muted cultural conflict with whites.[17]

What Underhill muted in Chona's life was told quite clearly by three Pomo women who spoke to Elizabeth Colson from 1939 to 1941. Their stories tell of white men kidnapping women and children, of Indian women killing infants born after forced sexual relations. Along with these bitter histories were recollections of childhood, descriptions of basketmaking, and accounts of cultural changes, such as when Indian women saw Japanese women picking hops, then went into the fields themselves.[18]

These Pomo stories, unusual in the directness with which the women described their lives and Colson transmitted them, are part of the storytelling tradition relatively unmediated by the Anglo transcriber. The Pomo accounts do not fit easily into the earlier literary traditions of storytelling, but neither do they fit into the tradition of anthropology being practiced by Anglo women in the early twentieth century. At that time Indian women were less likely to write about themselves than were Anglo women, who began to assert themselves in the developing anthropological literary tradition.

The anthropological literary tradition had its origin in the writings of tourists and of amateur archaeologists and ethnologists. Like historians and sociologists, anthropologists moved into the academy and professionalized their field at the end of the nineteenth century, establishing regular classes and whole departments devoted to the study of anthropology. These early academic anthropologists developed a new anthropological literary tradition. They mandated that writing about native peoples be based on actual observation and that the results of that observation be embedded in an objective style that distanced the writer from the subject. When anthropology students began to go into the field in the first decade of the twentieth century, few had the freedom to remain for extended periods of time. Their academic advisers sometimes helped them to obtain financing to remain in the field for several months; they also expected the students to shift to whatever culture the advisers thought deserved observation. Most anthropology teachers expected their students to ask the questions that the teachers wished to have answered and to impose a non-Indian framework on the stories collected. Anglo women who went into the field during the next two decades followed this method.

The transition from travel account to anthropological monograph was a slow one. Travel accounts, which tended to describe the present, were often written by upper-middle-class women just passing through an area. Charmian London's *Voyage of the Snark*, describing her journey with Jack London to the South Pacific, was published in 1915. Such popular adventure stories may have whetted the appetite of middle-class Anglo women to observe and describe exotic native cultures. But the new systematic and scholarly disciplines of anthropology, archaeology, and ethnology excluded women. Matilda Stephenson, who came to the southwest in 1879 with her husband to explore native cultures in New Mexico, organized women in separate professional organizations and insisted they had the right to join scholarly discourse.[19]

In the early twentieth century anthropologists scorned descriptions of changing cultures and their struggles to survive as "salvage" anthropology. They searched for Native peoples who appeared to have intact cultures. They abandoned a study of cultures that emphasized history, change, and similarities to Anglo cultures, searching instead for pattern, structure, and difference. They stressed observation and interrogation of informants in the field rather than written archival materials. As anthropologists moved closer to the native cultures, they distanced them in their writings.[20]

Nancy J. Parezo writes that before World War II more than sixteen hundred women worked with and published articles on Native Americans in the greater Southwest alone. My sampling of almost fifty women who conducted fieldwork informally or who were formally trained in anthropology is thus only a small part of the large group of women who wrote about Indian women in the West during the years from 1900 to 1940. They ranged from Grace Nicholson, the Pasadena trader who collected but never published her field notes, to Ruth Benedict whose book *Patterns of Culture* sold tens of thousands of copies. Most Anglo women anthropologists came to the Southwest as professional, trained observers to foreign lands. At first they were tourists in a strange land, coming for a short time, describing the cultures they saw as practitioners of a profession dedicated to the systematic, rather than casual, description of exotic cultures. Gradually, many of these women established roots in the Southwest, either moving there or returning each summer.[21]

Local Anglos, as well as Indians, were skeptical of the ability of the first newcomers to accurately describe the Indian cultures they knew. Mary B. Watkins sent Grace Nicholson a detailed description of an Indian ritual held by the Mesa Grande people of southern California. "The Berkeley Prof.," Watkins wrote wryly, was there for a few days and then went back to write a thesis full of mistakes. Watkins even complained that Constance DuBois, not a Berkeley professor but a self-trained ethnologist and careful observer, tried to make the facts fit the theories of people who knew nothing. And yet Watkins had no time to write from her years of close observation. "It is the too many tasks, and my dearest work must be left for the last." Evaline Nelson, a woman living in Orleans, California, wrote to Nicholson in 1916 that she had collected information about her Indian neighbors all her life, planning to tell her sons who she expected would publish a book. But the sons died and she lost her ambition to pass on the information. "I absorbed, as it were, all I saw and heard and today if I had the command of the English language I could do lots more, could tell you more were I not handicapped for the lack of it."[22]

Women who tried to go into the discipline without formal aca-demic training had difficulty being accepted. Constance DuBois, the woman Watkins said fit facts to theories, had financing from Phoebe Hearst and encouragement from Alfred Kroeber, chief anthropologist at the University of California, Berkeley. But lack of formal training kept her from joining fully in the anthropological literary tradition.[23]

Native American women had almost no chance of joining this group who studied Indian peoples. Ella Cara Deloria, the Yankton Dakota who attended Oberlin College and then Columbia University, seems to have been the only Indian woman to be accepted as a practicing anthropologist. Indian women in the Southwest who wrote about their cultures never gained recognition. Emma Reh, probably Navajo, wrote at least two articles. One on peyotism was published under the name of an Anglo anthropologist. The second, an account of Navajo foodways that was prepared for the Soil Conservation Service in the 1930s, re-mained unpublished until 1983.[24]

Even with education, networks, and the support of powerful men, women writing Southwest anthropology during the 1920s and 1930s required extraordinary vitality, persistence, and strategy. To receive for-mal training at the Ph.D. level remained difficult through the first half of the century, and prejudice against women in the field lingered into the 1970s. Between 1894 and 1939 Harvard graduated no women among fifty-three anthropologists at the Ph.D. level; the University of Chi-cago had two women among thirty doctoral students between 1897 and 1940. The University of California at Berkeley, with fairly open graduate programs, graduated only nine of twenty-seven from 1901 to 1940. Franz Boaz, and particularly Ruth Benedict from 1920 to 1940, offered support for women and accepted them as intellectual equals at Columbia University, where women gained twenty-two of fifty-one Ph.D. degrees in anthropology between 1901 and 1940. But even Benedict, as powerful as she was within the profession, was passed over for promotions. In 1931 Lila O'Neal became the first woman to teach anthropology at the University of California, Berkeley.[25]

The women who made their way into this carefully controlled professorial elite gained great privilege at the same time they suffered continued discrimination. Women could speak, but only in an echo of the male voice—which precluded telling the stories of Southwest women in their own voices or accurately reflecting the culture by sharing the Indian women's lives.

The anthropological form itself enforced a kind of conformity. The accepted style dictated that anthropologists remove themselves from their stories. Women were powerfully positioned to reflect on the roles of women in both cultures, but they seldom did. Two formally trained African American anthropologists were able to transcend the anthropological detachment and speak in a different voice. Katherine Dunham, who studied Haitian dance, published her experiences in a popular form, in addition to the monograph that she carefully prepared for her dissertation. Zora Neal Hurston wrote the novel *Their Eyes Were Watching God.* The writing by most trained anthropologists was not, as Deborah Gordon says of Hurston, "neutral, unique, and transcendent." To validate their new field as a respected area for cultural discourse, most women had to establish their literary authority by removing the author from the story and concentrating on the experiences of the informant.[26]

In their writings anthropologists often made Indian women's lives invisible. Authors such as Ruth Bunzel, who focused on women's art, seldom placed that art in the context of women's lives or the community. Ruth Underhill's *Autobiography of a Papago Woman* transmitted the voice of an Indian but little about her life in the Tohono O'odham or Anglo communities. Anglo women left the stories of the women themselves only partially told.[27]

One must turn to later, less carefully crafted accounts to find the stories neglected in the earlier anthropological literary tradition. Esther Goldfrank, for example, described the "little company of progressives" at Laguna who worked with anthropologists from 1917 to 1920. Margaret Eckerman, the daughter of a Laguna mother and an Anglo father, kept house, cared for six children, and interpreted for the visiting anthropologists. Her family became the major informants. Jennie Day Johnson boarded anthropologists and introduced them to informants. Jennie, Goldfrank remembered, gave the impression of "self-confidence and capability" and had a neat comfortable home with a sewing machine. The Laguna village, Goldfrank recalled, had a "lot of Albuquerque furniture, cheap prints, tin roofs, and ruffled petticoats ripped up for bed sheets." Stores sold bread, candy, bottled drinks. At Laguna the women used Spanish hornos (outdoor adobe ovens); bartered bread and chili to Navajo men for jewelry and rugs; bought calico, shoes, stockings, shawls, and silk handkerchiefs. Some spoke English and maintained a correspondence with the foreigners whom they had welcomed into their homes. Jennie Day said she owned two of her household's rooms and could rent them without consulting her husband. Another time Goldfrank stayed with an Indian postmistress. In Goldfrank's accounts we see glimpses of busy women taking the time to care for early visiting scholars, helping them to buy objects, and furnishing them with access to cultural artifacts. They also worried about whether their telling secrets would lessen the power of their culture and whether the information would be used by the anthropologists to make money.[28]

Goldfrank's descriptions of Cochiti and Isleta are just as vivid. At Cochiti, Isabel Diaz termed herself one of the "progressives," spoke English to Goldfrank, worked with her on kinship terms, and helped her rout bugs from the bedroom. Goldfrank also referred to being assaulted by the teenage son of another family at Isleta and routing him with a good swift kick. In the rambling, grumbling, contradictory style of Goldfrank, these women and their families become real. In fact, that is part of the basis for Goldfrank's quarrel with Ruth Benedict. Pueblo women were not all alike. Some moved back and forth between different cultural positions. The patterns here are not smoothly consistent, but broken and changing.[29]

Goldfrank and the Pueblos shared the same time and place in a period when the Pueblo cultures were growing and changing. The cultures were not distant, but immediate, comforting, *and* threatening. Studies that impute to other cultures boundaries that separate values as timeless, not affected by their own time, create culture gardens, says Johannes Fabian. These gardens are surrounded by walls that the ethnologist goes behind where time is different. Goldfrank did not create these exotic culture gardens. Her cultures grew, blended, and changed in the same time.[30]

Goldfrank spoke in a different voice from other anthropologists. She opened her prose to the autobiographical style. Carobeth Laird did the same thing in her book *Encounter with an Angry God*, where she described her relations with anthropologist John Peabody Harrington and with informants. Their voices moved closer to the actors, departing from the ethnographic present of the anthropologists. It had a directness that was different from the voice of the conventional anthropologist and different from the voice of the early twentieth-century travelogues, in which women wrote of foreign cultures for curious middle-class folk who could not venture to exotic lands. Laird eventually ceased entirely to be an anthropological traveler, marrying her Chemehuevi informant, George Laird, and settling with him in Poway near San Diego.[31]

In only a few books did anthropologists show the confusion of the present. Because the observer was part of the story in these books, the text was less filtered, telling the reader more about the cultures and the anthropologists who viewed them. Fabian argues that anthropology patrols the frontier of Eurocentric cultures, is concerned with boundaries, and provides arranged and ordered knowledge. But the views of Goldfrank and Laird roam along the borderlands where cultures meet rather than patrol. These works of Goldfrank and Laird are not so important as analyses, but they remind us of the process of being the observer. They allow us to know the subject, to go behind the mask of anthropological method—a mask that confined the women anthropologists of the early twentieth century even as it allowed them to participate in a literary tradition.[32]

The rich lore of anthropologists contrasts sharply with the general lack of writing by and about ethnic women and working-class Anglo women. While the oral tradition persisted, these were stories without a written text; unlike Quintasket, few women wrote or found others willing to record their stories. And as the frontier literary tradition took form, it omitted Indian women as writers of these stories. A few pioneer stories by Anglo women were published in the early nineteenth century, and far more after the 1890s. But the bulk of pioneer autobiographies were not published until after 1920. Many remained family stories, kept in manuscript form by descendants; very few poor women left any accounts at all. Those who did hardly dared tell their true histories before the 1920s. Women simply did not tell their life stories for publication.[33]

Nor was the avant-garde literary tradition well developed until the 1920s. That some western women did publish experimental writings

made them extraordinary. In *The Yellow Wallpaper* Charlotte Perkins
Gilman wrote about her mental breakdown, but it was published as
fiction in 1891 and only in 1913 did she acknowledge the story as based
on her own experience. Gertrude Atherton's stories of wild western
women shocked easterners, but she remained reticent about her own
life. Mary Austin began to write about women's personal conflicts, but
could find no tradition that allowed her to speak openly about the experiences of western women. Zoë Akins set most of her comedies in an
upper-middle-class living room, usually in the East. The pull of romanticism also made it difficult for women to write about their own lives.
Even in the 1920s those women, like Gertrude Stein, who left America
to became professional writers in Europe deeply encoded their personal
lives in avant-garde writings. The experiences of two Anglo working-
class women—Anne Ellis and Agnes Smedley—illustrate the problems
western women faced during the 1920s and 1930s when they wished to
tell the stories they knew best—their own.[34]

The idea that she could write did not even occur to Anne Ellis
until she was almost fifty and in ill health. Then it took her seven years
to write and publish *The Life of an Ordinary Woman*. Born in 1875,
Anne lived most of her life in mining camps in Colorado. She had a
mother who could neither read nor write. Her father had "a good education for those times" and wrote for some popular magazines, but his
main talent, Anne remembered, was "getting ready to do a thing." He
wandered off and finally divorced her mother who cooked, sewed, and
cared for the two young children. Her mother married a second time,
bore five more children, and died. Abandoned by the father, Anne, the
eldest, married, leaving the younger children to care for each other.
Anne outlived two miner husbands and raised her children alone, sewing, cooking, and eventually running for political office. Asthma brought
on by overwork put her in a sanitorium in Albuquerque.[35]

In 1919 Anne went to a women's political meeting, where she wrote,
"I met a charming woman wearing the most Indian jewelry I'd ever
seen on one person." The woman was Inez Cassidy, from whom Anne
rented a room in Santa Fe several years later. One night when writers
and artists gathered around the Cassidy fireplace eating toast, quince
jelly, and hot chocolate with whipped cream, Anne told stories of her
experiences in the old mining camps. Cassidy encouraged her to write
them down. "Everyone in Santa Fe has either a brush or a pen in hand—

sometimes both," Ellis wrote. "They urged me to try to write and suggested—since I didn't know the first thing about it—to write it to Mrs.
Cassidy in the form of letters. Now I could neither spell, punctuate, nor
write a clear sentence, but how I wished I could!—and, being the sort
of a person who will try anything once, the very next morning before
daylight, I began my story."[36]

Ellis had read constantly during her life. Borrowing most of the
books and grabbing minutes between sewing and cooking, she read
everything from Shakespeare and Dickens to Nick Carter adventure
books. When she saw an ad in the *Women's Home Companion* for "My
Lady's Library," which came with a shelf to hang on the wall and a
place to hang cups underneath, she eagerly paid eleven dollars a month
to acquire the library.[37]

Ellis eventually wrote three books, all of them while she was bed-
ridden. "I wrote, then warmed my cold, cramped hands underneath the
covers, and wrote again," she said. Inez Cassidy was not enthusiastic
about those first numb-fingered attempts. Nevertheless, she encouraged Ellis to continue, and after "the best month in my life," Ellis left
Santa Fe with "the most compelling driving, hopeful, soul-satisfying
interest I was or am ever to know."[38]

The next summer Ellis wrote in every spare moment. She sent
samples to Cassidy who at first did not respond, then simply told her to
keep writing. Frantic to know if she could write, Ellis sent sketches to
magazines. Editors rejected them and advised she try something else.
Anne's sister warned her to keep the story of their lives to herself, but
she did not. In Oroville, California, where she went to try to recover
her health, she rented two small rooms in a "not very good district,"
coughed all night, read and typed all day, and in the evening went out
and stole roses.[39]

Ellis sent the finished manuscript to Cassidy on 1 May 1925. Cassidy
took the chapters with her to New York and wrote an encouraging
letter to Ellis. When the New York editors said they wanted the manuscript rewritten from letters to a narrative form, Ellis did so, meanwhile
receiving more rejections from journals who found her stories "too sad"
or "not significant." The public did not want such ordinary stuff, wrote
one editor. Cassidy's New York publisher never even replied to Ellis.[40]

Sick, lonely, and often cold, Ellis wrote on for the pleasure it gave
her. She wrote in the San Luis Valley of Colorado, where she still had

her home, in California where she visited her sister, and in New Mexico where she attempted to recover her health and cure her severe attacks of asthma. In Santa Fe, Mary Barrego, who worked for Cassidy, rented her a house and urged Mary Austin to visit. Austin brought Ellis home-made apple jelly and a rose geranium leaf in a jar. Ellis just grew sicker, going into the hospital finally, and then home.[41]

The search for health and a publisher continued into 1928. Al-most four years had passed since Ellis had begun to write on her tablet in the cold Santa Fe mornings. What she wanted was only enough to live in a modest house in a warm place. Ellis appealed to Julia and Royce Armstrong, a wealthy couple in Evanston, Illinois, to "grubstake" her while she was searching for a publisher. The Armstrongs had met Ellis in Colorado when they were on a horseback trip. They lost their way and wandered into the camp where Ellis was cooking for a con-struction crew and reading *Hamlet* in the cook tent. Ellis sent a copy of the manuscript to the Armstrongs, asking for their help again, this time in finding a publisher. Julia Armstrong sent the manuscript to a suc-cessful writer, Lucy Fitch Perkins, who read portions to "discriminating listeners." She passed the manuscript on to Houghton Mifflin editors and on December 24, 1928, they accepted the book.[42]

We may never know what was in the original manuscript. Houghton Mifflin had Kathleen Carman Dodge edit, rearrange, and shorten it. After restoring some parts, Ellis approved the final manuscript. The book was published in August 1930. Two weeks passed; then, Ellis wrote in a later book, "the letters began to pile in and haven't stopped to this day—interesting, appreciative, astounding, wonderful letters.... And the reviews! Oh, my friends, those reviews were worth living for!"[43]

Ellis wrote and finally published because a widening group, prima-rily but not exclusively women, sustained and supported her efforts. They cared for her, encouraged her, found others to encourage her, sent money, searched for publishers, and finally convinced Houghton Mifflin to publish and edit her books. They allowed Anne Ellis to speak for herself, to write for herself.

Too ill to sustain a career, Ellis nonetheless published two more books, one in 1931 and another in 1934. In them she described her political career in Saguache County, Colorado, and her efforts to write and to get well. Ellis died in 1938 at age sixty-three. She had written one story—her own. And it allowed readers to learn about the life of an ordinary western woman who viewed her hard life with humor and straightforward pride in work.[44]

For Ellis the pioneer literary tradition worked. She found a small group of listeners and then a larger public. Other western women also wrote, but the multitude of silences are appalling. Each woman began by herself a literary journey she did not know others had taken. Giving voice to what they saw and felt was made more difficult by the lack of intellectual centers and support networks in the West, and those who wrote often did so by going elsewhere. Of the many Asian women who settled or were born on the West Coast during the early twentieth century, few wrote of their experiences. Canadian-born sisters Edith and Winnifred Eaton left an impressive number of writings about American women's experiences in the early twentieth century as both struggled to find a voice to express their Chinese mother's heritage. Edith, writing as Sui Sin Far, embraced that Chinese heritage and wrote of her racial consciousness and pride. Winnifred assumed a Japanese identity, used the pen name Otono Watanna, and avoided writing about her own past. Winnifred, looking back on her long and successful writing career, regretted she had written so much "sentimental moonshine" and betrayed her heritage. Nevertheless, in the novel *Cattle* she was able to show in stark terms some of the abuses by Anglo male ranchers.[45]

As historians dig deeper into the literary traditions of the West, they are finding more women who wrote. Mary Oyama and Hisaye Yamamota, Japanese Nisai women, wrote fiction and nonfiction in the 1930s, exploring interracial relations, interethnic prejudice, and gender-role expectations. But they wrote only intermittently and were silenced by World War II. Jade Snow Wong, who was born in Oakland and grew up in California, wrote her autobiography in the 1940s. She complained of silences imposed from inside and outside her Chinese cultural traditions. For Wong, silence was imposed literally by a father who made her keep silent except to repeat Chinese history lessons.[46]

Hispanas in New Mexico who could legitimately claim centuries' old pioneer traditions on the Indian-European borderlands, found it difficult to find and claim the pioneer literary tradition as their own. Instead of writing about the difficulties their cultures encountered during the recent past, they often looked to upper-class traditions to validate themselves and history. Carmen Gertrudis Espinosa, Aurora Lucero-White Lea, Nina Otero-Warren, Cleofas Jaramillo, and Fabiola

Cabeza de Baca published short stories and books, but they seldom wrote openly of their own experiences. They did affirm Hispano culture and document its history. These women began to reclaim their pioneer cultural territory and implicitly to challenge Anglo cultural authority. Confident of their control of English, they were conscious of themselves as bicultural, aware of the importance of maintaining Hispano culture and the Spanish language. Fabiola Cabeza de Baca's voice reclaimed a cultural heritage and built an identity that forcefully confronted both Anglo and Hispanic cultures. She wrote with little institutional support, few literary networks, and only intermittent help from family and friends.[47]

Turning from the pioneer literary tradition that Anne Ellis found to the avant-garde literary tradition that Agnes Smedley discovered, we see a similar process of finding a voice. Like Anne Ellis, Agnes Smedley grew up in the mining towns of the West. *Daughter of Earth* chronicled her move from a farm in Missouri to the western mining towns, then to California, New York, and finally to Europe. It was a personal and revealing book, made possible by the distance, physical and mental, she had traveled from the West. That she wrote it at all was due to a supportive literary group. Smedley began her public writing for the school newspaper at the Normal School in Tempe, Arizona, when she was seventeen. One of her first articles was a careful description of San Francisco's Chinatown. With her interest in other cultures, Smedley might under other circumstances have become an anthropologist. Instead she did clerical work in the West, then moved to New York where she worked for the Socialist newspaper the *Call*. She studied Asian history and philosophy on her own and in her spare time worked with a group of Asian Indian immigrants who were urging Indians to revolt against British control. In 1919 she moved to Germany to continue work with the Asian Indian nationalist movement there and in 1929 planned to go to India to work for Indian independence. Barred by the British from entering India, she went instead as a reporter to China, where she became famous as a chronicler of the Chinese Communist revolution.

In 1924, while living in Berlin, Smedley began to write about growing up in the Southwest. When the psychoanalyst who had advised her to write tried to seduce her, Smedley was not able to return to him for treatment or to continue the novel. Smedley received encouragement from anarchist Emma Goldman and money from birth control advocate Margaret Sanger, who urged her to continue writing. The Danish author Karin Michaelis invited Smedley to visit her home on an isolated island, and with a new analyst Smedley began to write again for the first time in nearly two years. During the summer of 1925 Smedley went to Denmark and finished the first draft in ninety days. Actress Tilla Durieux supported Smedley financially while she finished the last revisions; she also convinced the *Frankfurter Zeitung* to publish the book in German.[48]

Smedley wrote openly about her life, but she was worried that her friends would shun her for that frankness. A middle-class American friend warned her it was "unethical" to expose her "sacred experiences" to the public and advised a pseudonym. Smedley published the book under her own name, but changed the names of the characters and altered some events. She chose the name Marie for the main character.[49]

The theme of the book is Marie's search for autonomy. The search grows in the course of the novel, which begins with her sense of security in rural Missouri, then describes the increasing difficulties of her family as they move to the mining camps of Colorado. Marie wants to excel at school, but as she grows older and the family poorer, as her father finds it more difficult to care for his family and spends more time in the saloon, Marie must go to work after school as kitchen help. Eventually, she helps her mother take in laundry, becomes one of the worst students in her class, and steals to help support the family her father has abandoned. Gradually, the mother, whom Marie hated as a child, becomes her champion in the quest for an education. Marie, in turn, becomes the mother's shield against the father. Marie goes from teaching to stenography school and finally to writing for a magazine. After a cowboy friend stakes her to six months of school, Marie becomes editor of the school newspaper. During the next years, Marie struggles to earn enough money to continue her studies and resists marriage and motherhood, which would interfere with her learning. Over the years, her search for sexual autonomy, writing skills, and political activism become intermixed. She marries an Indian political activist. When her personal and political lives become too complex, her writing suffers. The tension between the desire to write and a husband who tells her she should not leads to illness and a decision to emigrate.

Smedley's book ends with Marie leaving the United States. Her story chronicles a western working-class woman's quest for the autonomy to learn and to write. Along the way many women and men help her—with money, with encouragement, by teaching her skills. According to Smedley's biographers, Janice and Stephen MacKinnon, however, the financial and emotional support she needed to actually tell her story came from small, intellectual avant-garde circles in Germany and America.

Smedley wrote *Daughter of Earth* in Europe in circumstances very different from Ellis's. Yet she too struggled to find not just a voice but also listeners. Smedley finished the English revisions and worked on a German translation of *Daughter of Earth* in the summer of 1928 and it was published in both languages. Smedley's American lawyer negotiated a contract with Coward McCann, a small American avant-garde publisher. In contrast to *The Life of an Ordinary Woman*, Smedley's book did not sell well. It probably sold fewer than five thousand copies in its 1929 English edition; a second, expurgated edition published in 1935 sold even fewer. Only as a Feminist Press reprint in the 1970s did *Daughter of Earth* find a mass audience. Feminist Press has sold several hundred thousand copies of the book and kept it in print for almost twenty years.[50]

The anthropological, pioneer, and avant-garde literary traditions fit imperfectly the desires of western women to write. The women almost accidentally joined these traditions at a particular time, gained some support, then ventured on, depending mostly on their own efforts to tell their stories. These were women who moved forward in their own ways, still muffling their voices, wearing masks that hid their own and other women's lives, but opening possibilities, giving voice to their stories. They managed, somehow, to find a place to grow, a place to write.

One can see gender, class, and ethnicity at work in complex ways to both restrict and encourage the voices of western women. On the whole, Indian women had relatively little help from Anglo-American men or women in telling their stories during the first half of the twentieth century. At a time when many Indian women were willing and able to relate their experiences, few Anglo-Americans were able to listen. Instead, like making baskets, stories became primarily something told within cultures and families, preserving them privately rather than publicly until a generation of college-educated children could begin the task of translation for a non-Indian audience. Nevertheless the women who did write and tell their stories provide a first generation of storytellers whose voices can still be heard. On the borderlands of their cultures, they translated and shaped stories that made parts of their cultures understandable for others. They began to reveal a tradition that later Indian women writers have shown to be powerful and transforming.

By default men rather than women usually helped early Indian women transmit their stories, because few Anglo-American women had opportunities to do so. When non-Indian women had opportunities, they were restricted by professional writing codes from exploring in written form relations with the Anglo-American world and certain subjects, especially sexuality—their own or that of Indian women. They did not write about the lives they shared with Indian women and men. Restrictions on their own sexuality and the need to live what Anglo-Americans called exemplary lives in public, constrained the way in which they could discuss Indian lives as well.

Two types of literature emerged, one popularized for children, another esoteric and specialized for professionals. Both shared characteristics of restricted range of sexuality. Women anthropologists wrote about others and other cultures, but not about themselves and their own cultures, although they were well situated to do this and to write about Indian women in new ways. The lives of women anthropologists are now being analyzed more carefully by other writers to reveal what was left privately in writings and through oral histories, but it is important, as these private voices are made more public, that we not forget how restricted the public discourse of women anthropologists was in the early twentieth century and how male canons in the profession determined how they would speak about themselves and others. As middle-class, educated women, their voices were heard, but only in particular ways. Most felt that their profession gave them opportunities unavailable elsewhere and the body of work they left as writers is testament to that reality. It is a unique, important body of work by middle-class Anglo-American women who explored the West in their writings in important if restricted ways. Because most were outsiders to the cultures of western women, at least initially, they were motivated to explain what they saw. It gave them an important though constrained role in speaking about the lives of some western women.

Like Indian women, working-class Anglo-American women found it difficult to tell their stories. They also had to seek middle-class assistance. Such assistance enforced their need to speak of gendered lives, to translate female experiences into a language understandable to a larger public of both sexes. They learned to explain region and class in acceptable ways for women and men who did not share those experiences. Their stories were most acceptable when they told of mothers who struggled to raise their children, like Anne Ellis; much less popular when they told of struggles to give form to childless lives, like Agnes Smedley. The process of giving life to their own experiences was constrained at best. For most working-class women, even Anglo-Americans, it was virtually impossible. Only access to small support groups of primarily upper-middle-class women who functioned as patrons made it possible for women to publish books. Most women of other ethnic groups, who lacked even this access, told their stories in oral form.

Sometime patronage was not the same as long-term support for careers as writers. These women remained sometime writers, who only rarely achieved regional, much less national success. Without national success, it was difficult for other writers, especially women writers, to even find that tradition. Without their own press, literary establishment, or easily accessible audiences, women of the West wrote each time into a vast cultural silence, never knowing whether what they had to write was reaching the people for whom it might begin to form a living tradition rather than just a historic episode. When they wrote of western cultures as an exotic past, they were most likely to find a national audience. Even then, a rural past—in whatever style, by members of whatever culture—was of decreasing interest in a country where the urban population was the most highly organized consumer of literature. The insurgent voice, speaking for those cultures against the authority of the dominant Anglo-American urban culture, was the least likely to be written, printed, read.

In order to write at all, women had to live at the margins of their own cultures, where a multicultural perspective allowed them to describe the West. Mary Austin claimed that the regional writers of the Southwest were preoccupied with landscape and peoples. Surely these writers shared such preoccupations, but more importantly, they were preoccupied with how to give voice to their experiences. Many women did break the silence to write, but the lack of small groups to listen to the many voices kept far more female voices from blooming out of the West. Not to have an audience was to die. Not to have a small audience who would help provide a larger audience was to remain almost as voiceless.

6

FROM THE BORDERLANDS
CREATING A MEMORY

Gloria Anzaldúa wrote in her 1987 book *Borderlands*:

To survive the Borderlands
you must live *sin fronteras*
be a crossroads.[1]

In this chapter, I turn to the question of how to think *sin fronteras*, to be a crossroads in our analysis of women as cultural workers in the twentieth-century American West. Anzaldúa has not only expressed the issues poetically but also grasped the political and intellectual importance of the positioning of women on these borderlands. Anzaldúa's *Borderlands* is a good place to begin seeing how scholars might position themselves as crossroads for historic memory.

Anzaldúa's concept of culture at the margins is based on her experiences as a Chicana *tejana* growing up along the borders with Mexico and the cultural borders of the Southwest. "I am," she wrote, "in all cultures at the same time," continually walking out of one culture and into another. As a mestiza, she felt caught in the cross fire among ethnic cultural camps as she moved from one to another. Moreover as a lesbian and a feminist, she felt in a sense she had no country, no race, no ethnic culture at all. She thus became a crossroads, taking up what she called the "Mestiza way." At this crossroad she hoped to reinterpret history and shape new myths: to inventory her ancestral heritage, mediate between cultures, share history, and voice needs.[2]

It is not the acknowledged role of scholars to create myths, but they do respond to them, and cultural myths certainly shape their work.

Scholars, like other cultural workers in the arts, both express and shape the social context that produces them. Memory emerges out of a combination of encounters with the material world and the ways in which various groups of people interpret those encounters. Conflicts over memory of the past usually indicate changes in the material world, interpretations of those changes, and projections of what they mean for the future. Thus the present and the future are always being commingled in the shaping of historic memory. One task of scholars is to be explicit about how this commingling affects their work and the work of others.

Scholars are by no means the only groups who shape historic memory. Oral traditions and popular traditions jostle the elite written memory that scholars usually produce. Oral traditions may coincide with the other two, but in the past have often receded from the public to the private sphere as Euro-American cultures expanded beyond direct contact among individuals. Popular traditions usually reach larger numbers of peoples and are often based on unconscious nostalgia about the past. Elite traditions develop out of the need for permanent elaborate records that extend beyond oral and popular needs and may be more conscious of nostalgia. Let me explain this trilogy of oral, popular, and elite traditions a bit more.

Before the spread of printing, the oral tradition played the most important role in what people remembered. I have been looking at a book on memory and how the European oral tradition of memory developed. Until the seventeenth century, the elite had elaborate ways to remember things they wished to speak about. For example, mental journeys through buildings—theaters or mansions of the mind—allowed people to store specific memories in specific localities in the buildings, to represent ideas they wished to recall. A later mental journey through the same theater of the mind could recall these ideas in total detail.[3]

The spread of printing made this oral tradition obsolete for most European men, but oral traditions continued in other cultures, which retained their own memory techniques. There were, and are, female cultural memories as well as male cultural memories, but we know little about them. When my students interview relatives for my women's history classes, they seem to tap into this memory: they bring stories so tragic that they cannot speak of them in class. We have few ways to systematically sample these memories, or the way events are selected and organized for remembering. The written literature of cultures that are still close to the oral tradition is very important because it taps into these collective memories and allows us to hear what has been passed down by women, often in languages other than English. American Indian, Mexican American, Black, and Asian women, as well as working-class white women, have preserved these traditions. This is itself cultural history, but we have to work from the present backward to recreate a more complete history from these complex and varied collective memories.[4]

Popular memory may take many forms and incorporate performing or visual arts. It is sometimes known as folk knowledge but it usually flourishes during periods and among groups who see the present as a decline from the past. Nostalgia may form a large component of this popular memory. Memory is used to sort out events of the past in search of confirmation that the past was indeed better than the present. This nostalgia for things past often brings lay people to the study of the past.

Women who participated in the rituals of nostalgia in their art were often the most successful. Nostalgia for the vanishing Indian was the basis for the success of artists Grace Hudson and Emma Freeman in the early twentieth century. When Zoë Akins and Agnes de Mille tapped into nostalgia for traditional male-female relationships, where women played stereotypical roles, they found wide audiences. Even Martha Graham used nostalgia to popularize modern dance. The American West is a favored locale for nostalgia, and all western artists have had to deal with that fact. To avoid confronting the easy comfort of nostalgia about the West, artists have often used their western base to see the East in different ways, but pictured the West in ways acceptable to easterners.[5]

In explaining the forms of nostalgia, Fred Davis points out that both popular and elite art use nostalgia, but in different ways designed for different audiences. Popular art tends to use simple nostalgia; elite art invites the audience to question the truth of nostalgic memory. Elite art uses various techniques to heighten awareness and develop for the audience a new relation to the past. In this way, nostalgia itself can become a way to use the past creatively.[6]

Whatever group dominates the re-creation of the past, controls the use of nostalgia. Some creative women themselves skillfully manipulated elite and popular nostalgia in their time. They themselves participated in nostalgic rituals that kept alive memories of past relations and obligations. Their nostalgia helped present continuity amid threats of discontinuity. To encode a consciousness of that nostalgia within a work of art took great ability. That consciousness was not always explicitly encoded. It might not be present at all in the cultural work, but only in the social context, either public or private, within which the work was created.[7]

Like individuals, societies wish to think well of themselves. Cultural workers are always having to come to terms with this fact. The younger the culture, the more mobile, and the more discontinuous, the greater the need for nostalgia. Nostalgia may reaffirm identities that are shaken and transcend differences. "Nostalgia reenchants," writes Davis, "if only for a while until the inexorable processes of historical change exhaust that past which offered momentary shelter from a worrisome but finally inexorable future."[8]

Gender plays an important role in nostalgia. Studies have shown that males have a greater need for nostalgia than women, especially when their status is most threatened. The current nostalgia for the mythical "ideal family" may reflect one such yearning. Women who feel threatened may also yearn for the past, though they seem to do so in fewer numbers, less often, and for different reasons than men. Men may yearn for a recent past because it seems a time when their domination was less contested, or a period farther in the past before the uncertainties of the marketplace. The mythical West often seems a perfect locale for both of these types of nostalgia. Women may yearn for a state of nature or youth, or another culture in which women seem less subordinate. Lately, some Western Indian cultures seem attractive alternatives because women had a central role in many of them. Today, women are less likely to use the recent past as a locale for nostalgia, because they often see real achievements in their lives.[9]

Creating new myths is not the same as nostalgia for the past, but new myths do need new ancestral protagonists. Here historical scholars perform an important function in providing ancestors and in analyzing the historical and cultural contexts within which they lived and worked. Scholars also provide syntheses that educate themselves and larger groups of people about how to "see" the past, what to look for, and how to look at it. Scholars tend our collective past—that garden of delights (and horrors)—acting as gate keepers, as pruners of memory, and as directors to paths they think seekers should take. They also quarrel with each other over how to manage their tasks.

These quarrels have preoccupied historians of the American West of late. One might expect reflections on how historians have written the history of the West to be inventories, a retelling to others of their historical journeys, and a thoughtful analysis of their own collective past. Historiography, the history of history, would seem to be the place for this inventory. But historiography has in recent years been dominated by fairly abstract theories about the philosophy of history, and so historians of the American West, in typically western fashion, have chosen to shoot from the hip in quite public spaces. This shootout has tended to take the form of a debate over what our white male western ancestors did and how historians should portray them. The battles have been fought out in the halls of Congress, in the major art museums, and on the pages of journals, both scholarly and popular. Collectively the battles are called the New Western History (NWH for short) debate.[10]

The most visible, national, and public of these debates occurred in the spring of 1991 when the Smithsonian Museum of American Art opened its exhibit *The West As America: Reinterpreting Images of America.* The curator of the exhibit, William Truettner, did not choose to revise the canon by including and reinterpreting the work of western women artists. Most of the painters he used to illustrate the exhibit were men, as were all but three of eighty-six biographies of western artists included in the catalog. Truettner's goal was to reinterpret the way in which visual artists used western landscape and people as a locale in which to embed nostalgia as an escape from present urbanization and industrialization, and to read the art objects themselves as reinforcing and freezing certain myths in the American mind.[11]

The Smithsonian's interpretation of western art was not entirely new. A father and son team, William H. and William N. Goetzmann, had published *The West of the Imagination* in 1986. This book referred to western art as image-making that had contributed to "the fundamental myth of the American experience—the story of the peopling of a vast new continent by immigrants from the old European world who were forever moving West." In the book and in an accompanying Public Broadcasting Station series, the authors talked about "our collective imaginations" and the "Tale of the Tribe." The Goetzmanns, like William Truettner, were applying a respected theory, that paintings can be seen as cultural objects in which individuals or groups assert their interests in pictorial language. In the hands of the Goetzmanns, the interests seemed fairly benign, a sort of folktale told through art. But the Smithsonian exhibit used public funds, a highly visible public space, and national treasures to explain nationalistic goals, a national mission, the colonization of the West. The exhibit decentered, analyzed, even psychoanalyzed, the content of the paintings and concluded not only that looking at the images of the West could tell us something about America but also that the message was not a glorious one. A number of western historians had been saying the same thing for some time, but not in such a prominent place.[12]

Given the way in which American culture was being appropriated in the growing political and ideological battles in the United States, no one should have been surprised at the negative response to the exhibit. For centuries the West had been the repository of a kind of national nostalgia. The exhibit threatened to take that away by asking viewers to see the images of the West in a negative political context. When the historian Daniel Boorstin visited the exhibit, he wrote in the guestbook that it was "a perverse historically inaccurate, destructive exhibit."[13]

The history of the West had taken on a new, or perhaps simply recurrent, place in national culture debates. Historians, like curators, had been experimenting with a history of the West that made it less accessible as a locale for nostalgia. Few of the New Western Historians questioned the importance of the West. They had, however, frequently embraced the Turner thesis, which emphasized the crucial role of the West in shaping the American character, in a new way. The West did affect the American character, these studies implied, but it did so negatively. It provided not an edenic landscape nor even a Wild West where white males (cowboys) easily triumphed over people of color (Indians), but a place where bitter conflicts over land and control reflected a conflict over the meaning of capitalism. These views soon became known as the New Western History.[14]

Western history had run into what is sometimes called postcolonialism. This is a position that views the expansion of the industrialized nations in terms of domination by white males and subordination of people of color and white women. While the focus is still on the white male, the implication is that white women and ethnic groups might have different stories to tell. And since these stories are being told now—in gendered and multicultural histories—the threat to "old western history" and to the national consciousness transformed what had been quiet academic debates to angry, loud, public exchanges.

Larry McMurtry, a highly successful historian of the West, spoke most forcefully and visibly against the New Western History. McMurtry had been an innovative manipulator of the contradictory images of the West. In *Lonesome Dove* he reinvested the old myth with new, more appropriate images, including those of women. He did not, however, interrupt the basic Anglo male nostalgia as had other historians and the curator of the Smithsonian exhibit. McMurtry dubbed the NWH— along with women studies and ethnic studies—as "trendy," in other words having no future. The NWH should be called "failure studies," he asserted.

The Smithsonian controversy and McMurtry's reaction to the New Western History confirmed that most people still regarded western history as more than just regional history. Western history was embedded deeply in the national culture, as a sort of psychic frontier where people could escape to avoid the problems of the present and the prospect of the future. Any attempt to restore women, including women artists, to this history had to come to terms with a proprietary claim that many people had on western history. They would not easily give up old interpretations— neither the central place white men have claimed in that history nor the conviction that it was ultimately a positive one. Historians searching for new ways to represent the West had to accept this fact.[15]

Women, men, white and colored, were all locked into this battle over the past, the present, and the future. These were, after all, battles for future consciousness about common ancestors who had different experiences. The battles were being played out in contemporary cultural shootouts. These shootouts at the gates of memory have been a distraction from evaluating just what has been accomplished by historians of women in opening new paths into the garden of history. Here we move from taking inventory to examining those repressive traditions that Anzaldúa wants to omit from the myth, which is crucial in creating space for new ancestors and a new consciousness of creative women as cultural workers in the West.

The new feminism of the 1960s is already more than thirty years old, which is time enough for historians of the recent past to see different themes emerge. These have affected the way in which historians have looked at the garden of history and the paths they have taken.

Some analysts already see three stages in this short history of women's history, stages that roughly coincide with the 1960s, 1970s, and 1980s. All three represent ways of interpreting the past, ways that continue to enrich our search for women who were cultural workers.

When historians began to write scholarly histories of women in the 1960s, they were a part of a present in which increasing numbers of newly affluent, educated, and mostly middle-class white women were demanding a new history that recounted their story, one that they saw was not being taught in the academies at which they were learning about what the historical scholars had codified as history.

The codification of history had taken place in this way. When Americans professionalized and specialized in the late nineteenth century, art historians and literary historians tended to stay within those disciplines. General historians—trained primarily to look at intellectual and political history—created their own separate academic discipline, called simply *history*. That history focused on small groups of eminent white males who had transformed the East and brave white males who had won the West. Responding to the political winds of the 1960s, many American students of history turned to social history, looking for new ways to explain what political and intellectual history had not given them, and for new ways to look at those who had been excluded from the old history. Intellectual and political history was abandoned by many younger historians of the 1960s because it did not seem to explain the experiences of most Americans.

As social historians reevaluated American history, they generally ignored intellectual history. Gradually, the old intellectual history became part of cultural history—the study of how cultures, elite and popular, are created. This history began to close the gap left by art, literary, and general historians by providing a scholarly memory of the process that chooses what is worth retaining as history. The growing field of feminist studies, which has given considerable attention to women's art and literature, when joined to this newly developing field of cultural studies, offered ways to help understand the process by which historians created a historic memory.

Intellectual history ran aground on its inability to respond to the new ways in which social history looked at the past. This can be described metaphorically as a sort of historical geology, a place where the fault lines, and hence the changes, seemed to run along the boundaries of gender, race and ethnicity, and class. Domination by the powerful majority over groups less powerful seemed to run along these lines that facilitated subordination. Changing material conditions, often created by the majority itself, stressed the fault lines, leading to further conflict and change. Social historians saw these fissures as important clues to how and when cultures changed. Because art and literature were not the special purview of historians and because politics and economics still seemed to be the focus of social controversy, historians ignored much of what had been the old intellectual history. Although academic historians contributed in a major way to reevaluating social, political, and economic history, they did not take the lead in critiquing or reforming the old intellectual history. It looked as though women, through exclusion, had not participated in the creation of elite cultures, although they might have participated to some extent in popular culture, especially as performers. There were just not many interesting questions to ask because there seemed to be no women there. Family, work, and politics offered more attractive areas for analysis.

The pruning of cultural history had to do partly with the process of selection by the male historians who composed the scholarly elite. In the search for patterns, for theories, even for a good narrative history, professional historians were taught to throw out almost everything from our diverse and complex past. What little they kept was called *history*. Pruning the historic memory was easiest when whole groups within a culture could be eliminated. The gatekeepers—those who determined the criteria for pruning—eliminated the study of entire cultures and concentrated on a few. Cultural gardeners then systematically pruned away Euro-American women, people of color, and most unprivileged white men. When admitted, these groups became "others," those inferior to and outside the bounds of "civilization." Usually, they were not admitted to a place in an intellectual past. This oversimplifies a bit, but not much.

This tradition of elimination had strong ideological underpinnings in European philosophy. Over the centuries, European theories of creativity narrowed the number of styles and practitioners considered geniuses. In a sort of cultural apartheid, the European tradition placed women outside the role of genius. By the end of the eighteenth century, philosophers linked genius to human creativity, which made humans resemble gods, made them superior to other creatures. Or rather some humans. Although creative women existed, they were excluded

from the realms of greatness by a logic that defined genius as male.
Men created art. Women created crafts. Likewise, indigenous peoples,
when encountered by European males, were defined as outside the male
tradition. They too were "others" who, by definition, created not art
but craft. Theories of creativity excluded popular, traditional, and ethnic art along with oral literature. What was left, an elite art, was handled
in a variety of ways. Creative territories became gendered, the author's
voice was insistently European and nonfemale in most cases. As these
ideas about creativity accompanied intellectual history, they were en-
sconced in nineteenth-century romanticism and rearranged in twentieth-century modernism.[16]

World War II seemed to revitalize these old theories about women
lacking the ability to be creative. Heightened nationalism, centraliza-
tion of government, and wealth in the 1940s was followed by a lower-
ing of the status of women in many areas of American life. Women had
always been active in creating both elite and popular culture, but as
more and more women seemed anxious to appropriate and shape elite
cultures, men seemed less willing to share that role. The result was the
revolt of young white middle-class women, who used the intellectual
and cultural tools at their disposal, a Euro-American cultural context
of modernism, a political context of civil rights, and an economic context of increasing wealth. All this terrain seemed to be male dominated. To establish a movement against male control, women began to
recruit other women. Feminism took its early form as a totalizing concept, which was common to modernism: all women were oppressed
because they were women. Men had drawn the lines at sex, excluding
women, and so women did the same. Men oppressed women because
they were women. All women shared this oppression and were equal,
thus sisters. Sisterhood was powerful. It could transcend differences in
the same way that male solidarity had seemingly transcended differences. Many historians emphasized the common experiences that
women had because they were "born female."[17]

Historians of women decentered men by supporting inclusion of
women, but to move from negative theories of oppression to those of
agency, scholars also began to look for women's culture. They discovered that history could be written in terms of differences. For example,
a tradition that excluded females also excluded female traditions in art,
unless they wrote or painted in appropriate styles.

Identifying female traditions was not an easy task. Naomi Schor saw one tradition as emphasizing "detail." She traced this tradition of detail in European art as a matrilineal one, passed on from female to female. It reached back to classical times and traveled alongside a dominant male tradition that devalued detail and stressed the ideal. Males abstracted and were idealists; women, in their attention to detail, sought to transcend this male world, according to Schor. She saw a constant struggle of women using detail against men who used ideas. There was, Schor implied, something essentially female about the tradition of "detail."[18]

Questioning the theory of exclusion also led, inevitably, to a search for exceptions. While women, in theory, should not have been artists, in practice some were. Early searches for women in the arts led to the discovery of a growing number of these exceptions to the theory, especially in the nineteenth and twentieth centuries, and a growing ability of some women to find a place in the collective memory we call history.

According to sociologists Gladys and Kurt Lang, the collective memory is formed by the artist, as well as by those who come after her. If she does certain things, she makes it easier to find a place in the collective memory. One cannot be exemplary if a place in the collective memory is too difficult to find. The Langs suggest that, for visual artists, reputation depends upon producing a critical mass of work, keeping adequate records to guarantee proper attribution, and making arrangements for proper custodianship. The artist has to leave behind a sizable, accessible, identifiable work and people with a stake in its preservation and promotion. Preserving and promoting was, of course, what women had frequently done for male artists, but which men had only rarely done for them.[19]

The first stage of the feminist movement attempted to find these lost cultural workers along with other historical women. As sex had become a criterion for exclusion, it now became a criterion for inclusion. Hence, the floor of names that accompanied The Dinner Party. The early feminists remembered these women in their floor, and museum exhibits influenced thousands of viewers, especially women. But the floor found no institutional space and no collective emotional support broad enough to retain it in public memory. Instead, women had to fall back on the space they had been most successful in appropriating, literary and academic space. A spate of exhibits of women's visual arts, some even of artists in the West, began to appear in the 1970s. These exhibits reinscribed the older idea that the arts must be exemplary and asked the question of why women had not been considered as exemplary or admissible to the canon, the collective memory passed on formally, in recent times usually through universities. The first stage of feminism challenged the old canon, scholars provided new models produced by Euro-American women, as well as a few women and men of color, and the canon began to recodify.

Criteria for selection among these new exemplars concerned some theorists. These could simply be selected as variations of mainstream themes, leaving assumptions intact. It could simply prune the old majority, and legitimize a new minority. *Making Their Mark,* an exhibit and catalog from 1989, later did this for contemporary women artists. The same was done for other creative genres, such as writing.[20]

Many feminists were not content with just separating out women because they were women. Feminist art, argued philosopher Hilde Hein, had to do something different. It had to depend on an aesthetics of experience. The road to theory had to be traveled through the particularity of women's lives. Because gender was socially constituted, it had to be contextual, "saturated with experience." To escape being ephemeral, it had to move from experience to reflection, but it must, Hein argued, stay close to the edge of its experiential source. Hein worried about adopting male language and truth-claiming. She wanted skepticism rather than reverence, reappropriation rather than submersion.[21]

This tension between critiquing the old canon and the new made feminist theory about the arts complex. Philosopher Anita Silvers argued that canonical works were exemplary and thought to persist in their successors. But if women's work had no history, if it continued to be dropped out of the canon, then it could not become exemplary. Thus, women's cultural work needed a history that both rediscovered and revalued it. That history had to explain why women's work was neglected—and why that neglect differed from the neglect accorded some male work. Feminists needed to analyze why, as Silvers said, "women have been disproportionately unable to create art which is accepted as enduringly exemplary." The reason is not that they had been categorically repressed; many did have popular success. Perhaps the art was neglected just because women created it. History had to gain more than just a room of one's own within the canon, said Silvers; it had to put women at the center of the scholarship. The canon, she argued, needed a history of its own.[22]

Without a separate history, a context for the arts, women artists would be like spare parts, available to be used by the mainstream to show diversity, without any basic change. In visual and literary arts, separatism seemed to be followed by selective mainstreaming, that is picking some new artists to include when they seemed to fit into a mainstream already shaped by the old canon. That seemed to end the issue for many, just as the first stage of political feminism seemed to be ended by legislation and integration. Women's history, however, had provided no place explicitly to develop and critique women's traditions in the arts.

The first stage of feminism did not exclude women of different classes and races. It explicitly attempted to include them. All women, regardless of their position in society, shared certain experiences and upon these experiences a political movement could be founded. The experiences, at first, tended to be expressed in cultural terms understandable and acceptable to young white middle-class women responding to the power of both young and elder white males who seemed to share power. The implication was that women were all alike.

By the 1970s critiques of this total position had emerged, primarily from women of color who claimed the right to interpret the content of feminism from their own perspective. The flaw seemed to be that early white feminists assumed that multiple experiences led to one perception of those experiences, that oppression could lead to unity. Instead, different experiences could be perceived differently and lead to different positions. Instead of feminism, theorists began to talk about feminisms. The modernist paradigm was breaking down among groups of women, not only those searching for political agendas and for women's history, but among cultural workers as a whole. The intellectual replacement of modernism was postmodernism, a cluster of ideas that had the capacity to once again rearrange the old theories to devalue women's creativity or to empower them by embracing the diversity of cultures. Scholarly women, who remained primarily white and middle class, were profoundly affected by the postmodern movement and participated in creating it. They did so not only because, like women of color, it challenged claims of some to speak for all, but also because it opened up new opportunities to accommodate those challenges and move to new, more flexible positions.[23]

The movement of Lucy Lippard, a feminist art critic during this transition, is one way to track this change. Lippard was born in 1937 in

New York City, raised in New York, Louisiana, and Virginia. By 1990 she listed her residences as New York City; Georgetown, Maine; and Boulder, Colorado. As both a writer and activist, she has responded to and helped shape both political and cultural history.

Lippard is known for her feminist essays on women's art. She began applying her feminist insights to aesthetics and politics in the 1960s and has moved constantly in new directions. In the 1960s she too was proselytizing for a public art, a broader art audience, and looking for sexual content in art. Males became targets for her revolt, not because they were males but because they were the authorities. But she advocated, even in the 1970s, the goal of feminist art to affect everyone, "all those people whom contemporary art has failed to reach or to move." Lippard was less concerned with women joining the mainstream than with their redefining and changing its direction by finding new audiences. That, she argued, was the most creative thing an artist could do. To accomplish this, she proposed strategies that could reach a mixed male and female audience as well as a separate female audience. She used a system of exchange as well as separation. She identified a female world, an art world, and a real world, and she wanted women to operate in all three.[24]

In *Mixed Blessings: New Art in a Multicultural America*, Lippard offered a model of how to bridge those worlds. Examining the themes of mapping, naming, telling, landing, mixing, turning around, dreaming, she moved toward looking at how cultures saw themselves and others, the way that cross-cultural activity was reflected in the visual arts. The book was primarily about younger or lesser-known artists and avoided master narratives and cultural myths. But it also avoided directly confronting old cultural myths. It was a patchwork of images that drew on feminist models of art that were relational and unfixed.

The result was a study focused on people of color, not through formal exclusion or inclusion, but because they had frequently "offered sanctuary to ideas, images, and values that otherwise would have been swept away in the mainstream." Lippard saw the borderlands not as a geographical space, but a place of cultural dialogue "porous, restless, often incoherent territory, virtual mine fields of unknowns for both practitioners and theoreticians." Her book was, she said, a book about our common "anotherness," and how we cross cultures. Hers was a shared present, a culture that included the entire fabric of life and a multicultural one that was also cross-cultural when various communities worked together. She was after that neutral territory Trinh Minh-ha talked of, the area in between, "where new meanings germinate and where common experiences in different contexts can provoke new bonds. It was what Anzaldúa would have called "the crossroads."[25]

Lippard was driven by the logic of feminism, postmodernism, and multiculturalism to a new place. None of these intellectual currents alone would have taken her to this position. Even together, without her desire to understand the politics of aesthetics, they might not have taken her so far. All seem to be necessary to fashion a new memory of the borderlands, that geographical space as well as the place of the mind that western women have occupied.

Although Lippard moved to new models for viewing contemporary arts, she did not settle the problem of a history of the arts. She valued the present, she said, because "Western Civilization" had so often claimed that present and relegated other cultures to the past. But such "presentism" avoided the issues of how that claiming and relegating of cultures occurred in the past. It provided no map of how that historical process continues to influence the present.

The new intellectual paradigm of postmodernism reclaims the present and allows it to become a crossroads, a borderlands. In the hands of other feminists, this 1970s critique of 1960s feminism resulted in a complex discussion of theory. Because cultural studies, especially study of western American women as cultural workers, will have to emerge into this intellectual world already occupied by discussions of theory, it is necessary to return to it again to understand how it may assist or impede that emergence.

During the postwar decades, postmodernism gradually shifted the way cultural workers perceived and described their worlds. As an era and a major intellectual shift, it can be seen as a response to the physical retreat of Europe in the face of external and internal postcolonial movements. It also was a determination to come to terms with an intellectual world that was responding to new global politics and economics. Postcolonialism from within took the form of women's and ethnic studies that challenged control of white elites, including class-based theories that had provided a major base for the dominant liberalism. Some theorists saw postcolonialism as the end to the concept of history as Europeans had known it since the Enlightenment of the eighteenth century. Intellectuals had focused on the past to show there had been change or progress in Europe in a rational chronological way. Maybe, some postmodernists theorized, history was random, ambiguous, irresponsible. At any rate, as we have seen, postmodernism called into question theories about progress, and as such interrupted those working with western American history as it did those studying Euro-American civilizations.[26]

American historians, particularly historians of women, began to rediscover intellectual history in the 1980s. Under pressure from other disciplines, historians now looked at what had been intellectual history as a part of social or cultural history. They began to ask how people had created this part of the culture, how intellectuals and artists had functioned in society, and how they participated in the creation of belief structures. When historians returned to the study of this part of history, they found that it had become the province of theories developed primarily from other disciplines, in literature, psychology, and philosophy, and that they were working from this cluster of attitudes, assumptions, and questions loosely defined as postmodernism.

This postmodernism contained two bundles of theories, as Jane Caplan calls them, that further complicated and really muddied the intellectual waters. These were poststructuralism and deconstruction. Both originated in European linguistic theories that loosened critical thought from external reality and described it as a total (sometimes almost totalitarian) system.[27]

Poststructuralist theories, when applied to the humanities and social sciences, demoted reality and elevated cultural systems that described how language gave meaning to reality. These theories tended to argue that one could not talk about objective reality, only the way people talked about it. It once again privileged ideas over objects. Most historians in the American West ignored these theories in the 1980s. They continued to write as though a reality existed outside language. Feminist historians in the West were more influenced by these theories because they often worked within women's studies, which had many younger scholars trained in the East or at elite western universities where these theories were popular.

Until the 1980s, few American feminist historians had to confront and apply poststructural theories. Most kept their eyes and pens on what they considered to be a real world in which women daily struggled.

Theories seemed less enticing than the "real" history feminist historians still perceived as important to women's struggle for liberation. In some ways, feminists did have to confront the implications of these theories because they rejected the total theories and dualistic theories of early feminism. If gender was not socially constructed as two systems, with all women sharing one, then feminist theory would have to be revised.

Deconstruction, a variant of poststructural theory, was much more immediately helpful to American feminist historians. It gave them a method of critiquing the texts that men had written, including those of poststructuralism, because it more insistently focused on the written text. The text was everything, but the readings were constantly shifting. Of course, historians had already given some attention to how to read texts, but deconstruction encouraged critical and systematic reflection on how they read texts, and provided a method for doing so.

As a method, deconstruction was extremely helpful in analyzing specific texts, but as a theory it was more problematic. The theory implied that historians should ignore analysis of society as a whole and focus on a self-conscious analysis of the texts that individuals had left. It deemphasized the context, the conditions that surrounded a text and within which the writer was positioned. In privileging written texts, it privileged the cultures of middle-class Euro-American men and women. Nonetheless, Caplan argued that these theories could open up a discussion about how exclusions were permitted and maintained. This discussion could allow assessment of all communication that excluded— not only written texts, but also other forms of communication used by women of different cultures.[28]

Deconstruction could thus become a valuable tool for creating a history of the arts because they employ signs that are enmeshed in socially constructed systems of meaning and value. Moreover, because history creates literary texts, it can be subjected to questions about what is valid historical narrative and who decides. Deconstruction could help override claims that history is exempt from the self-questioning that has occurred in the other humanities. Thus, a basket created by Joseppa Dick and the way it made its way into the marketplace and museum might function as well as a written text in finding out about the past. It might also lead us to more careful reflections on how we "read" that text and context, and why Indian arts were not included in the writing of history.[29]

Nevertheless the possibilities for a cultural history have come burdened with the debates over theory. If the debates do not explicitly exclude women as women, they do exclude those who do not wish to or are unable to participate in the new discussions because of limited access to the means of communication. The old modernist metanarratives had explicitly excluded subordinated groups, but literacy in English could offer access. The new postmodernism seemed to exclude even those with literacy because it imposed a new hurdle of a highly specialized language, a jargon. Those who had mastered this special language could discuss theory, those who had not were excluded.

One response was to abandon all theory. Some feminists advocated abandoning generalizations about gender and how it was socially constructed, even in its diverse forms. Such a position would just leave many experiences, making political as well as intellectual judgments all relative. This could allow more monolithic and traditional theories to flourish unchallenged, and allow social realities to be ignored.[30]

Women of color had a more telling critique of theory. They were the first to specify exactly what seemed to result from this new elevation of theory and its exclusiveness. Nina Baym pointed out that theory could encourage diversity, a creative dancing, but it also could impose uniformity, an enforced march. Literary theories could simply be applied to texts already sanctioned by the academy, even if the accepted texts had been expanded from those formally published works of women to less formal, often unpublished letters and diaries. Norma Alarcón pointed out that even if texts by women of color were included in the canon, if they were excluded from the theory they would be silenced once again. Tey Diana Rebolledo argued that theory about texts could even interfere with focusing on the text itself. "We have talked so much about theory we never get to our conclusion nor focus on the texts. By appropriating mainstream theoreticians and critics we have become so involved in intellectualizing that we lose our sense of our literature and therefore our vitality."[31]

If theory were compatible with feminism, or even feminisms, why did these women of color feel it was exclusionary? Maria Lugones wrote about feminists becoming "world-travelers"; Trinh T. Minh-ha, about differences being used as a tool of creativity to question forms of domination, creating a ground that belonged to no one; Anzaldúa, about that "consciousness of the borderlands," a sense of being on both shores at once, of crossing cultures. It seemed that women of color were to continue carrying the burden of cultural critique, expanded now to include feminists as well. Barbara Christian complained of the attempt to deconstruct the literary tradition of northern industrialized nations and to substitute philosophical writings for literary ones. She warned that feminist theorists might even be concentrating on the politics of theory in order to avoid the new postcolonial literature being written by women of color. "Writing disappears unless there is a response to it," wrote Christian. Thus theory could preempt the writings of women of color.[32]

Others realize that in a world of theory, feminists too must have theory. Writer bell hooks has tried to rescue feminist theory by arguing that "any constructive examination of feminist scholarship and its political implication must necessarily focus on feminist theory." For hooks, feminist theory is something to be struggled over, not ignored. She sees a kind of feminist theory that strengthens the feminist movement by being "liberatory," that synthesizes the most visionary feminist thinking, that is directed at the masses—women and men—to educate them collectively for critical consciousness. Academic theorists still seemed to be producing a "Eurocentric, linguistically convoluted" theory rooted in "Western male sexist and racially biased philosophical frameworks" that promoted academic elitism, and an anti-intellectual and antitheoretical bias that women had been conditioned to accept by male traditions. Still, she argued, all theory emerged from abstraction and all people abstracted about their daily experiences. The goal then, should be to explain this abstraction in more accessible language.[33]

Many women of color did provide abstractions about daily experiences in more accessible forms to broad audiences. They combined storytelling, poetry, and history with feminist criticism. Most found that alternative feminist, ethnic, and university presses were most receptive to their writings, but even mass publishing establishments opened to their work. One problem is that these are most accessible through the medium of print at a time when print itself is becoming more expensive and specialized. The cultural fragmentation to which postmodernism is a response is also caught in those fragments. That the language of the theory is inaccessible may not matter; it will speak to small, highly educated groups of intellectuals. But the patterning characteristic of modernism is being repeated: we broaden the numbers of exemplars from whom we choose, but we still exclude. More could still mean less.[34]

Now what are the implications for creating a memory from the borderlands? What guidelines can assist cultural workers who write the history of other cultural workers in occupying the crossroads? It is from this perspective that I offer a few last points about creating a memory from the borderland.

First of all, before entering our garden of delights (and horrors), we must recognize current social reality. Today, that reality seems to be that as the global economy takes form women are increasingly heading households, that a two-tier class system is emerging. At the top a gender-mixed and ethnically mixed work life is possible, whereas at the bottom a disproportionately high number of women and men of color are being left with no waged work life at all and decreasing access to the many means of communication. These social realities should increase our attention to how culture both reflects and influences social realities; but it should also cause us to reflect on how our own work affects the present and engages the future as well. Feminism must still be basically political, grounded in a theory of social agency and resistance.[35]

When we prune the gardens of the past, we must be particularly attuned to the different forms that cultural history takes in different cultures. Diverse experiences and diverse means of communication, both elite and popular, are important in cultural representation. We need to include examples from this diversity and to move back and forth between what is sometimes called public and private history.

I think that we cannot strengthen our analysis by avoiding theory. We need to examine self-critically the ways in which theory is necessarily embedded in our own work. We also need to explicitly ground our theory in historical social reality, situate it within historical frameworks that are based on women's lives. These frameworks must include a discussion of those lives that were excluded in the past through theories as well as through practice. We need to know who was dominant and who was subordinate, who challenged these categories, and how.

Which brings me back to the West, the "out there" with which I began these explorations in the history of women and creativity. For those engaged in the humanities, the task is to reevaluate women's multicultural past with both theory and detail. Otherwise, we will not know it. Women will again disappear from the record instead of enlarging their place in it.

I used to be fond of saying that women were central to history and had to be there at the center of our stories as well. Now I think the story is more complicated. Change takes place in various ways, frequently growing from the margins outward. I still like the concept of Anzaldúa's mestiza who stands as a crossroads for many cultures, who moves along the border between cultures, who sees the West as America, but who tells her story in many languages, in story and in song, to whatever audiences will listen to her clear strong voice. Culture is not something for the few to possess among themselves. It is the shared story of all the people who have created it. And we who are the chroniclers should listen, draw strength, and try to tell that story as clearly and strongly as we can to as large an audience as we can reach.

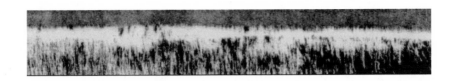

Notes

Introduction

1. Isadora Duncan, *My Life* (New York: Boni and Liveright, 1927), 340–41. The paperback version, which is still in print, has the same pagination.
2. Jane Jacobs, *The Death and Life of Great American Cities* (New York: Random, 1961); and Robert Venturi, *Complexity and Contradiction in Architecture* (New York: Museum of Modern Art, 1966), 16. For the history of the term postmodern, see Margaret A. Rose, *The Post-Modern and the Post-Industrial: A Critical Analysis* (Cambridge: Cambridge University Press, 1991), especially 3–20, 101–3.
3. Ibid., 11–12.
4. Ibid., 101–9.

1: Out There, Out West

1. The standard introduction to the Pomo is still the collection of articles in Volume 8 of the *Handbook of North American Indians*, ed. R. F. Heizer (Washington, D.C.: Smithsonian Institution, 1978), 274–305, by Sally McLendon and others.
2. Gene Weltfish, *The Origins of Art* (Indianapolis: Bobbs-Merrill, 1953), 172, 176–78. For various interpretations of the dau, see S. A. Barrett, "Pomo Indian Basketry," *University of California Publications in American Archaeology and Ethnology* 7 (1908): 133–276; Alfred L. Kroeber, "California Basketry and the Pomo," *American Anthropologist* 11.2 (1909): 233–49; and Barbara Winther, "Pomo Banded Baskets and Their Dau Marks," *American Indian Art Magazine* 10.4 (1985): 50–57.
3. John Hudson Field Notebooks, (20016) 1903, Grace and John Hudson Papers, Grace Hudson Museum, Ukiah, Calif. Hereafter cited as Hudson Papers.
4. Duncan, *My Life*. I have not footnoted quotes used in the following summary.
5. Ntozake Shange, *Ridin' the Moon in Texas: Word Paintings* (New York: St. Martin's, 1987), xi. See also Claudia Tate, "Ntozake Shange," in *Black Women Writers at Work*, ed. Claudia Tate (New York: Continuum, 1983), 149–74; Carol P. Christ, "i found god in myself...& i loved her fiercely: Ntozake Shange," in *Diving Deep and Surfacing: Women Writers' Spiritual Quest* (Boston: Beacon, 1980), 97–117; and Carolyn Mitchell, "'A Laying on of Hands': Transcending

the City in Ntozake Shange's *for colored girls who have considered suicide/when the rainbow is enuf*," in *Women Writers and the City: Essays in Feminist Literary Criticism*, ed. Susan Merrill Squier (Knoxville: University of Tennessee Press, 1984), 230–48.

6. Ntozake Shange, *for colored girls who have considered suicide/when the rainbow is enuf: a choreopoem* (New York: Collier, 1989 edition), ix–xii. All page references are to this edition. The original edition was published in 1976 by Shameless Hussy Press, San Lorenzo, Calif.

7. Ibid., x, xii. Ann Halprin was an important Bay City dancer who developed choreography for finding the artist in ordinary people. See Sally Banes, *Terpsichore in Sneakers: Post-Modern Dance* (Boston: Houghton Mifflin, 1980), 8–9.

8. Shange, *for colored girls*, xi.

9. Ibid., 4.

10. Ibid., 42.

11. Ibid., 42–3.

12. Ibid., 45.

13. Ibid., 49.

14. Ibid., 51.

15. Phyllis Hoge Thompson, "This is the Story I Heard: A Conversation with Maxine Hong Kingston and Earll Kingston," *Biography* 6.1 (winter 1983): 6. For other important discussions see King-Kok Cheung, "'Don't Tell': Imposed Silences in *The Color Purple* and *The Woman Warrior*," *PMLA* 103.2 (March 1988): 162–74; Reed Way Dasenbrock, "Intelligibility and Meaningfulness in Multicultural Literature in English," *PMLA* 102.1 (January 1987): 10–19; Margaret Miller, "Threads of Identity in Maxine Hong Kingston's *Woman Warrior*," *Biography* 6.1 (winter 1983): 13–33; Maxine Hong Kingston, "Cultural Mis-readings by American Reviewers," in *Asian and Western Writers in Dialogue*, ed. Guy Amirthanayagam (London: Macmillan, 1982), 55–65; "Maxine Hong Kingston: The Woman Warrior," in James Craig Holte, *The Ethnic I: A Sourcebook for Ethnic-American Autobiography* (New York: Greenwood, 1988), 113–18; Suzanne Juhasz, "Maxine Hong Kingston: Narrative Technique and Female Identity," in *Contemporary American Women Writers*, ed. Catherine Rainwater and William J. Scheick (Lexington: University Press of Kentucky, 1985), 173–89; Stephanie A. Demetrakopoulos, "The Metaphysics of Matrilinearism in Women's Autobiography: Studies of Mead's *Blackberry Winter*, Hellman's *Pentimento*, Angelou's *I Know Why the Caged Bird Sings*, and Kingston's *The Woman Warrior*," in *Women's Autobiography: Essays in Criticism*, ed. Estelle C. Jelinek (Bloomington: Indiana University Press, 1980), 180–205; and Suzanne Juhasz, "Toward a Theory of Form in Feminist Autobiography: Kate Millett's *Flying* and *Sita*; Maxine Hong Kingston's *The Woman Warrior*," 221–37, in *Women's Autobiography*, ed. Jelinek.

16. Thompson, "This Is the Story I Heard," 11–12.

17. *Body/Culture: Chicano Figuration* (Rohnert Park, Calif.: Sonoma State University, 1990), 18; Amalia Mesa-Bains, "Quest for Identity: Profile of Two Chicana Muralists based on Interviews with Judith F. Baca and Patricia Rodriquez," in *Signs from the Heart: California Chicano Murals*, ed. Eva Sperling Cockcroft and Holly Barnet-Sanchez (Venice, Calif.: Social and Public Art Resource Center,

1990), 76–82; and Diane Neumaier, "Judy Baca: Our People Are the Internal Exiles," in *Making Face, Making Soul: Haciendo Caras: Creative and Critical Perspectives by Women of Color*, ed. Gloria Anzaldúa (San Francisco: an aunt lute foundation book, 1990), 256–70.

18. "Interview with Judy Baca," by Amalia Mesa-Bains. Archives of American Art, Smithsonian Institution, Southern California Archives, San Marino, Calif., 7–9.

19. Ibid., 10–11.

20. Ibid., 15.

21. Ibid., 13.

22. Neumaier, "Judy Baca," 258–59.

23. Ibid., 260.

24. Mesa-Bains, "Interview with Judy Baca," 4.

25. Ibid., 51.

26. Paula Gunn Allen, *Grandmothers of the Light: A Medicine Woman's Source Book* (Boston: Beacon Press, 1991).

27. Gayatri Spivak, *The Post-Colonial Critic: Interviews, Strategies, Dialogs*, ed. Sarah Harasym (New York: Routledge, 1990). See also the discussion in Laura E. Donaldson, *Decolonizing Feminisms: Race, Gender, and Empire-Building* (Chapel Hill: University of North Carolina Press, 1992).

28. bell hooks, *Yearning: race, gender, and cultural politics* (Boston: South End Press, 1990).

29. Gloria Anzaldúa, *Borderlands/La Frontera: The New Mestiza* (San Francisco: aunt lute books, 1987), 53–64.

2: An Energy of Their Own

1. Virginia Woolf, *A Room of One's Own* (San Diego: Harcourt Brace Jovanovich, 1989; reprint of 1929 edition).

2. S. A. Barrett, "Material Aspect of the Pomo Culture," *Bulletin of the Public Museum of the City of Milwaukee 20*, part 2 (1952): 402–3; and Sherrie Smith-Ferri, "Basket Weavers, Basket Collectors, and the Market: A Case Study of Joseppa Dick," *Museum Anthropology* 17.2 (June 1993): 61–66.

3. John Hudson to Grace Hudson, 10 January 1901 (4410), Hudson Papers. Searles R. Boynton, *The Painter Lady: Grace Carpenter Hudson* (Eureka: Interface California Corporation, 1978), 26 discusses numbering of 684 paintings. Reproductions are on 157–84.

4. Smith-Ferri, "BasketWeavers, Basket Collectors, and the Market," 61–66.

5. Barrett, "Material Aspect of the Pomo Culture," 401–2.

6. Smith-Ferri, "Basket Weavers, Basket Collectors, and the Market," 61; Sally McLendon, "Collecting Pomoan Baskets, 1889–1939," *Museum Anthropology* 17.2 (June 1993): 61–66; and Dorothy K. Washburn, "Dealers and Collectors of Indian Baskets at the Turn of the Century in California: Their Effect on the Ethnographic Sample," *Empirical Studies of the Arts* 2.1 (1984): 51–74.

7. S. A. Barrett, "The Ethno-Geography of the Pomo and Neighboring Indians," *Publications in American Archaeology and Ethnology* 6.1 (University of California, 1908), 48–50, 168–69.

8. Ibid., 168–69.

9. John Hudson to Grace Hudson, 12 February 1903 (43558), 2 May 1901, Hudson Papers.

10. John Hudson to Grace Hudson, 6 February 1903, Hudson Papers; and Smith-Ferri, "Basket Weavers, Basket Collectors, and the Market," 64.
11. Boynton, *The Painter Lady*, 183.
12. Helen Carpenter, "A Trip Across the Plains in an Ox Wagon, 1857," in *Ho for California! Women's Overland Diaries from the Huntington Library*, ed. Sandra L. Myers (San Marino, Calif.: Huntington Library, 1980), 93–188. See also Boynton, *The Painter Lady*, 3–11.
13. Carpenter, "A Trip across the Plains," in *Ho for California!* ed. Myers, 13–18.
14. For the change in the East see Kathleen D. McCarthy, *Women's Culture: American Philanthropy and Art, 1830–1930* (Chicago: University of Chicago Press, 1991), 70, 85, 99, 105.
15. Raymond L. Wilson, "Introductory Essay," in *A Woman's Vision: California Painting into the Twentieth Century*, 30 November 1983 through 31 January 1984 (San Francisco: Maxwell Galleries, 1984), 4–7. See also Isobel Osborne Field, *This Life I've Loved* (New York: Longmans, Green, 1937).
16. Phil Kovinick, *The Woman Artist in the American West, 1860–1960* (Fullerton, Calif.: Muckenthaler Cultural Center, 1976), 1, 4, 13, 26, 38, 58.
17. Boynton, *The Painter Lady*, 19–26.
18. Ibid., 157–64.
19. John Hudson to Grace Hudson, 9 February 1903 (435A-D), Hudson Papers.
20. John Hudson to Grace Hudson, 29 April 1905 (4381A-D), Hudson Papers. Grace painted one numbered picture in 1891, three in 1892, eleven in 1893, nine in 1894, and twenty in 1895. See Boynton, *The Painter Lady*, for lists.
21. John Hudson to Grace Hudson, 30 May 1905 (4388A), Hudson Papers.
22. Grace Hudson to John Hudson, 10 February 1901, 12 March 1901, in Boynton, *The Painter Lady*, 55–56.
23. John Hudson to Grace Hudson, 27 April 1901, Hudson Papers.
24. John Hudson to Grace Hudson, 21 May 1901, Hudson Papers.
25. Boynton, *The Painter Lady*, 56–57.
26. John Hudson to Grace Hudson, 9 September 1901, 7 October 1901, 12 October 1901, Hudson Papers.
27. Elizabeth Colson, *Autobiographies of Three Pomo Women* (Berkeley: Archaeological Research Facility, Department of Anthropology, University of California, 1974; reprint of 1956 edition), 21.
28. Boynton, *The Painter Lady*, 39–40.
29. Ibid., 79–80.
30. Peter E. Palmquist, *Camera Fiends and Kodak Girls: 50 Selections by and about Women in Photography, 1840–1930* (New York: Midmarch Arts Press, 1989), ix, 29–40, 181–84, 203–6, 217–24. For a critique of this fantasizing by Anglos, see Barbara Babcock, "By Way of Introduction," *Journal of the Southwest*, 32.4 (winter 1990): 400–437, and "'A New Mexican Rebecca': Imaging Pueblo Women," *Journal of the Southwest* 32.4 (winter 1990): 383–99.
31. Peter E. Palmquist, *With Nature's Children: Emma B. Freeman [1880–1928]—Camera and Brush* (Eureka: Interface California Corporation, 1976), 20–21, 36.
32. Ibid., 21–23.
33. Ibid., 24–26.
34. Ibid., 25–26.

35. Ibid., 28.

36. Ibid., 32–37.

37. Ibid., 20–21, 36.

38. Ibid., 41–47.

39. Ibid., 53.

40. Ibid., 54.

41. Gladys Engel Lang and Kurt Lang, *Etched in Memory: The Building and Survival of Artistic Reputation* (Chapel Hill: University of North Carolina Press, 1990), 187, 195–96, cite Helen Loggie of Washington and Helen Hyde of California as examples of printmakers who were successful during the postfrontier period. The Langs also believe that mutuality benefited women artists, although they discuss mainly partners who are artists.

3: Naming a Price, Finding a Space

1. There is no study of the trade in Native American baskets although numerous books exist on the art. Sherrie Smith-Ferrie, Anthropology Department, University of Washington, is completing a dissertation on the trade in Pomo baskets, which will be of major importance in helping understand the California trade in general. My generalizations are drawn from a great many sources. The best general works on Southwest basketry are Clara Lee Fraps Tanner, *Indian Baskets of the Southwest* (Tucson: University of Arizona Press, 1983) and Andrew Hunter Whiteford, *Southwestern Indian Baskets: Their History and Their Makers* (Santa Fe: School of American Research Press, 1988). On Pomo baskets see Sally McLendon and Brenda Shears Holland, "The Basketmaker: The Pomoans of California," in *The Ancestors: Native Artisans of the Americas*, ed. Anna Curtenius Roosevelt and James G. E. Smith (New York: Museum of the American Indian, 1979), 103–29. The Chetinasacher in Louisiana stopped making baskets early in the twentieth century because they could find no local demand and did not know how to develop a distant market through shipping. Mary Bradford to Grace Nicholson, 18 November 1906, Box 1, Grace Nicholson Papers, Huntington Library, San Marino, California. Hereafter cited as Nicholson Papers.

2. The special issue of the *Journal of the Southwest* 32.4 (winter 1990), "Inventing the Southwest" discusses much of the history of this trade. See especially Marta Weigle, "Southwest Lures: Innocents Detoured, Incensed Determined," 499–540 and Nancy Parezo, "A Multitude of Markets," 563–75.

3. McLendon and Holland, "The Basket-maker," 103–29, discusses some of these problems.

4. 1906 Diary, Box 16, Nicholson Papers; John Hudson to Grace Hudson, 25 March 1901, 27 April 1901, Hudson Papers. The best introduction to this ruthlessness in collecting is Sally Price, *Primitive Art in Civilized Places* (Chicago: University of Chicago Press, 1989).

5. John Hudson, "Pomo Basket Makers," *Overland Monthly*, 2d series, 21 (June 1893): 565.

6. Ibid., 562.

7. John Hudson to Grace Hudson, 7 January 1893 (43428), 12 January 1893 (4348A–C), Hudson Papers; Hudson, "Pomo Basket Makers," 564.

8. George Green to Grace Nicholson, 3 July 1940, Box 3, Nicholson Papers.

9. For Mary Benson see McLendon and Holland, "The Basketmaker," 112. For efforts to secure materials see John Hudson to Grace Hudson, 12 February 1893 (43558), Hudson Papers; and George N. to Walter Person, 9 May 1923, Box 3, Nicholson Papers.

10. Elsie Allen, *Pomo Basketmaking: A Supreme Art for the Weaver* (Happy Camp, Calif.: Naturegraph, 1988), 11–13. Originally published in 1972.

11. Family and Building Papers, Box 12, Nicholson Papers.

12. The only published discussion of Grace Nicholson's collecting is in Sally McLendon, "Preparing Museums for Use as Primary Data in Ethnographic Research," New York Academy of Sciences, *Annals*, 376 (1981): 201–27.

13. C. S. Hartman, "Values of Indian Baskets," undated, Box 14, Nicholson Papers.

14. Rayna Green, American Indian Women, talk given at New Mexico State University, 5 March 1991.

15. Summary Report on the Grace Nicholson Collection, Nicholson Papers.

16. Grace Hudson to Grace Nicholson, 19 June 1930, Box 4, Nicholson Papers.

17. Grace Hudson to Grace Nicholson, 9 December 1927, 5 April 1932, 10 August 1930, Box 4, Nicholson Papers. Richard Maxwell Brown, "The New Regionalism in America, 1970–1981," in *Regionalism and the Pacific Northwest*, ed. William G. Robbins, Robert J. Frank, and Richard E. Ross (Corvallis: Oregon State University Press, 1988) discusses the surges of regionalism, but not the responses of the East that Hudson seems to be responding to.

18. W. Jackson Rushing, "Marketing the Affinity of the Primitive and the Modern: René d'Harnoncourt and 'Indian Art of the United States,'" in *The Early Years of Native American Art History: The Politics of Scholarship and Collecting*, ed. Janet Catherine Berlo (Seattle: University of Washington Press, 1992), 191–236.

19. Grace Nicholson to Grace Hudson, 19 June 1930, Box 4, Nicholson Papers.

20. William Booth to Mary Austin, 1 November 1904, Box 85, Mary Austin Papers, Huntington Library, San Marino, California. Hereafter cited as Austin Papers.

21. See also Karen S. Langlois, "Mary Austin and Houghton Mifflin Company: A Case Study in the Marketing of a Western Writer," *Western American Literature* 23 (summer 1988): 31–42; and Karen S. Langlois, "A Fresh Voice from the West: Mary Austin, California, and American Literary Magazines, 1892–1910" 69.1 (spring 1990): 22–35.

22. James Watson to Mary Austin, 22 October 1921, 4 November 1921, Box 74, Austin Papers.

23. H. H. Howland to Mary Austin, 17 June 1925, 2 September 1925, and D. L. Chambers to Mary Austin, 2 October 1925, Box 64, Austin Papers.

24. Ferris Greenslet to Mary Austin, 25 January 1928, Box 85, Austin Papers.

25. Ferris Greenslet to Mary Austin, 19 May 1926, Box 85, Austin Papers.

26. T. M. Pearce, *Mary Hunter Austin* (New York: Twayne, 1965), 51, 54; Pearce, *The Beloved House* (Caldwell, Id.: Caxton, 1940), 195–205; and Anne Ellis, *Sunshine Preferred* (Lincoln: University of Nebraska Press, 1984; reprint of 1934 edition), 153.

27. Helen Peters, "Madonna of the Trail," *New Mexico Magazine* 71.12 (December 1993): 53.

28. Marta Weigle and Kyle Fiore, *Santa Fe and Taos: The Writer's Era, 1916–1941* (Santa Fe: Ancient City Press, 1982), 13–14; Kenneth Dauber, "Pueblo Pottery

and the Politics of Regional Identity," *Journal of Southwest*, 32.4 (winter 1990): 581.

29. Suzanne Baizerman, "Textiles, Traditions, and Tourist Art: Hispanic Weaving in Northern New Mexico," (Ph.D. diss., Department of Design, Housing and Apparel, St. Paul, University of Minnesota, 1987), 76–79, 130–31.

30. For the Hispanic women authors, see Tey Diana Rebolledo, "Las Escritoras: Romances and Realities," in *Paso por aqui: Critical Essays on the New Mexico Literary Tradition, 1542–1988*, ed. Erlinda Gonzales-Berry (Albuquerque: University of New Mexico Press, 1989), 199–214; and Genaro Padilla, "Imprisoned Narrative? Or Lies, Secrets, and Silence in New Mexico Women's Autobiography," in *Criticism in the Borderlands: Studies in Chicano Literature, Culture, and Ideology* ed. Hector Calderón and José David Saldivar (Durham, N.C.: Duke University Press, 1991), 43–60. Sarah Deutsch, *No Separate Refuge: Culture, Class, and Gender on an Anglo-Hispanic Frontier in the American Southwest, 1880–1940* (New York: Oxford University Press, 1987), 188–91, also describes the problems of "traditionalism."

31. Series of letters in box 64 from various Bobbs Merrill editors, Austin Papers.

32. Esther Lanigan Stineman, *Mary Austin: Song of a Maverick* (New Haven: Yale University Press, 1989), 192–93.

33. Greenslet to Austin, 23 November 1928, 1 February 1929, 13 December 1932, 28 February 1933, Box 87, Austin Papers. For the new tradition of women as literary artists see Elizabeth Ammons, *Conflicting Stories: American Women Writers at the Turn into the Twentieth Century* (New York: Oxford University Press, 1991).

34. Weigle and Fiore, *Santa Fe and Taos*, 35, 44.

35. Ibid., 129–36, last quotation on 136.

36. Henry Goddard Leach to Austin, 9 August 1928, Box 77, Austin Papers.

37. Barbara Buhler Lynes, *O'Keeffe, Stieglitz, and the Critics, 1916–1929* (Ann Arbor: UMI Research Press, 1989), 284–85, 305.

38. Ibid., 340 n. 23; Roxana Robinson, *Georgia O'Keeffe* (New York: Harper and Row, 1990), 299. On the cala lily hoax see Charles C. Eldredge, *Georgia O'Keeffe: American and Modern* (New Haven: Yale University Press, 1993), 25.

39. Robinson, *Georgia O'Keeffe*, 326.

40. Ibid., 339.

41. Ibid., 349–51.

42. Ibid., 382–401.

43. Ibid., 402–12, 423, 426.

44. Ibid., 428.

45. Zoë Akins to Alice Kauzer, 26 October 1939, Box 14, Zoë Akins Papers, Huntington Library, San Marino, California. Hereafter cited as Akins Papers.

46. Ronald Albert Meilech, "The Plays of Zoë Akins Rumbold," (master's thesis, Ohio State University, 1974), 1–2, 308. In a biographical sketch sent to Mr. Epstein [ca. 1930], Box 8, Akins Papers, she discusses why she went to California in 1907, how she produced her first play, and the influence of southern California on her life.

47. Zoë Akins to Alfred Vanderbilt, 16 March 1939, Box 24; Zoë Akins to Monty, 8 July 1935, Box 18, Akins Papers.

48. Zoë Akins to Alice Kauzer, 30 April 1939, Box 14, Akins Papers.

49. Correspondence is in Boxes 13–16, Akins Papers.

50. McCarthy, *Women's Culture*, charts this change.
51. Rushing, "Marketing the Affinity of the Primitive and the Modern," 191–236. For other discussions of the Indian art market see J. J. Brody, "The Creative Consumer: Survival, Revival, and Invention in Southwest Indian Arts," *Ethnic and Tourist Arts*, ed. Nelson H. Graburn (Berkeley: University of California Press, 1976), 70–84; Edwin L. Wade, "The Ethnic Art Market in the American Southwest, 1880–1980," in *Objects and Others: Essays on Museums and Material Culture* (Madison: University of Wisconsin Press, 1985), 167–264; and Nancy Parezo, *Navajo Sand Paintings on Boards: From Religious Art to Commercial Art* (Tucson: University of Arizona Press, 1983).
52. Peter H. Hassrick, "Western Art Museums: A Question of Style or Content," *Montana: The Magazine of Western History* 42 (summer 1992): 24–39.
53. Akins [to Thomas Prewitt], 29 February 1940, Box 21; Akins to Una [Birch], 14 February [1959], Box 20; and Akins to Dorothy Thompson [1959], Box 23, in Akins Papers.
54. Whiteford, *Southwestern Indian Baskets*, 133–41, 173–76.
55. See, for example, Lang and Lang, *Etched in Memory*, which discusses the market success of Helen Hyde, 195–96.
56. The best examples of this are in Gerald D. Nash, *Creating the West: Historical Interpretations, 1890–1990* (Albuquerque: University of New Mexico Press, 1991).

4: The Hungry Eye

1. Tillie Olsen, *Silences*, (New York: Dell, 1989; reprint of 1978 edition), 44.
2. Hal Foster, "What's News," *Village Voice Literary Supplement* 99 (October 1991): 25.
3. Elsie Allen, *Pomo Basketmaking: A Supreme Art for the Weaver* (Happy Camp, Calif.: Naturegraph, 1988 edition), 13–14.
4. "Interview with Susan Billy," by Sandra Metzler with Dot Brovarney, 5 August 1989, Mendocino County Museum, Willets, California.
5. Ibid.
6. Lawrence W. Levine, *Highbrow, Lowbrow: Emergence of Cultural Hierarchy in America* (Cambridge: Harvard University Press, 1988), 198.
7. William H. Goetzmann and William N. Goetzmann, *The West of the Imagination* (New York: Norton, 1986), 91.
8. The histories of these transitions are likely to be partial and told from the standpoint of Anglo enthusiasts. Nevertheless the merging of various influences to create new audiences, as well as artists, can be traced in such books as Kathlyn Moss and Alice Scherer, *The New Beadwork* (New York: Abrams, 1992).
9. Claire R. Farrer, "Singing for Life: The Mescalero Apache Girls' Puberty Ceremony," in *Southwestern Indian Ritual Drama*, ed. Charlotte J. Frisbie (Albuquerque: University of New Mexico Press, 1980), 126; and Cecile R. Ganteaume, "White Mountain Apache Dance: Expressions of Spirituality," in *Native American Dance: Ceremonies and Social Traditions*, ed. Charlotte Heath (Washington, D.C., National Museum of the American Indian, 1992), 65–81.
10. Charles H. Lange and Carroll L. Riley, eds., *The Southwestern Journals of Adolph F. Bandelier, 1880–1882* (Albuquerque: University of New Mexico Press, 1966), 374; Stineman, *Mary Austin: Song of a Maverick*, 174–75.
11. Anna Peterson Royce, *The Anthropology of Dance* (Bloomington: Indiana University Press, 1977), 130, 146–47 shows the continuation of this tradition

at Pow Wow dances. For Sioux at wild west shows, see L. G. Moses, "Indians on the Midway: Wild West Shows and the Indian Bureau at World's Fairs, 1893–1904," *South Dakota History* 21.3 (fall 1991): 205–29.

12. Clement Meighan and Francis A. Riddell, *The Maru Cult of the Pomo Indians: A California Ghost Dance Survival* (Los Angeles: Southwest Museum, 1972), 28–33, 111–15; Abraham Halpern, *Southeastern Pomo Ceremonials: The Kuksu Cult and Its Success*, Anthropological Records, vol. 29 (Berkeley: University of California Press, 1988), 28–34. "Dream Dances of the Pomo," a 1964 documentary, shows Pomo women dancing the Bole-maru, a blend of Christian, traditional, and reform dances. See *Native Americans on Film and Video*, ed. Elizabeth Weatherford (New York: Museum of the American Indian/Hayne Foundation, 1981), 39–40. The Bole-maru began after the Ghost Dance movement of the 1870s had already incorporated the traditional Kuksu dances and the reform Ghost dances. The antiwhite element was absent, but the dance is a strong statement of female power.

13. David Dempsey with Raymond P. Baldwin, *The Triumphs and Trials of Lotta Crabtree* (New York: Morrow, 1968), 233.

14. R. Hartley, "History of Dance in San Francisco," typescript chronology, San Francisco Performing Arts Library and Museum, San Francisco, California.

15. "Charles Quitzow and Sulgwynn Boynton Quitzow: Dance at the Temple of the Wings. The Boynton-Quitzow Family in Berkeley," (an oral history conducted by Suzanne Riess and Margaretta Mitchell, Regional Oral History Office, University of California Berkeley, 1973, 2 vols.), vol. 1, 43–49.

16. Mama [Mrs. Durrant] to Maud Allan, 1 February 1904, copy in Maud Allan Collection; "Maud Allan," typescript manuscript by Felix Cheriavsky, 1982, San Francisco Performing Arts Library and Museum, San Francisco, California.

17. Agnes de Mille, *Martha: The Life and Work of Martha Graham* (New York: Random House, 1991), 21–24; and Elizabeth Kendall, *Where She Danced: The Birth of American Art-Dance* (Berkeley: University of California Press, 1979).

18. Gayle Gullett, "City Mother, City Daughters, and the Dance Hall Girls: The Limits of Female Political Power in San Francisco, 1913," in *Women and the Structure of Society: Selected Research from the Fifth Berkshire Conference on the History of Women* ed. Barbara J. Harris and Jo Ann K. McNamera (Durham, N.C.: Duke University Press, 1984), 149–59. Maya Angelou, *Singin' and swingin' and gettin' merry like Christmas* (New York: Random House, 1976), describes the 1950s clubs.

19. Hartley, "History of Dance in San Francisco," San Francisco Performing Arts Library and Museum, San Francisco, California.

20. Nicolas Kanellos, *A History of Hispanic Theatre in the United States: Origins to 1940* (Austin: University of Texas Press, 1990); De Witt Bodeen, "Dolores del Rio was the First Mexican of Family to Act in Hollywood," *Films in Review* 18.5 (May 1967): 266–83; and Chris Strachwitz with James Nicolopulos, *Lydia Mendoza* (Houston: Arte Publico Press, 1993) all chronicle the transition from women's music in the home to public performances.

21. Dunham has not yet told the story of her professional life, but descriptions of discrimination are in "Katherine Dunham," *Black Writers: A Selection of Sketches from Contemporary Authors* (Detroit: Gale Research, 1989), 165; and in Agnes de Mille's patronizing essay of Dunham in *Portrait Gallery* (Boston: Houghton Mifflin, 1990), 38–50.

22. Lynne Fauley Emergy, *Black Dance in the United States from 1619 to 1970* (Palo Alto: National Press Books, 1972), 252–57. Duncan, *My Life*, p. 340 contains her fears of jazz.

23. Martha Graham, *Blood Memory* (New York: Doubleday, 1991); and Deborah Jowitt, *Time and the Dancing Image* (New York: Morrow, 1988), especially 167–233. On Graham see also de Mille, *Martha*, and Kendall, *Where She Danced*.

24. David W. Stowe, "Jazz in the West: Cultural Frontier and Region During the Swing Era," *Western Historical Quarterly* 23.1 (February 1992): 53–57, concentrates on the 1930s, but it is clear that jazz was being played in the West, as well as in the East, to large audiences in the 1920s.

25. Agnes de Mille, *Dance to the Piper & And Promenade Home: A Two Part Autobiography* (New York: De Capo, 1980; reprint of 1951 edition), vol. 1, 282–306.

26. de Mille, *Dance to the Piper*, vol. 2, 34–41.

27. Diana Crane, *The Transformation of the Avant-Garde: The New York Art World, 1940–1985* (Chicago: University of Chicago Press, 1987); and Serge Guilbaut, *How New York Stole the Idea of Modern Art: Abstract Expressionism, Freedom, and the Cold War*, trans. Arthur Goldhammer (Chicago: University of Chicago Press, 1983).

28. Kovinick, *The Woman Artist in the American West, 1860–1960*, 1.

29. Thomas Albright, *Art in the San Francisco Bay Area, 1945–1980: An Illustrated History* (Berkeley: University of California Press, 1985), 4, 11–12.

30. Ibid., 19; and Joan Brown Oral History, Archives of American Art, Smithsonian Institution, Microfilm Reel 3196, 35.

31. Caroline A. Jones, *Bay Area Figurative Art, 1950–1965* (Berkeley: University of California Press, 1990), 165 n. 44.

32. Ibid., 147; and "Leading Ladies: June Wayne, Claire Falkenstein, Helen Lundeberg, Joyce Treiman, Beatrice Wood," in *Yesterday and Tomorrow: California Women Artists*, ed. Sylvia Moore (New York: Midmarch Arts, 1989), 156–57, 163–67.

33. Ruth Azawa, "Art, Competence, and Citywide Cooperation for San Francisco," (an oral history conducted in 1960 and 1961, Regional Oral History Office, University of California, Berkeley, 1968); California Commission on the Status of Women, *Women in the Visual Arts* (mimeographed report of public hearing, Los Angeles, 24 February 1978): 17. See also Kathy Zimmer, "Silken Threads and Golden Butterflies: Asian Americans," 179–92; and Betty Kaplan Gubert, "Black Women Artists in California," 193–201, both in *Yesterday and Tomorrow*, ed. Moore.

34. California Commission on the Status of Women, *Women in the Visual Arts*, 18–19, 60. There is a year-by-year breakdown between 1963 and 1974 only for the California School of Fine Arts, later renamed the San Francisco Art Institute. It was 8 percent in 1968 and 12 percent by 1973. The California College of Arts and Crafts, which emphasized fields in which women had traditionally dominated, was 32 percent in 1974. Of 33 faculty in the Art Department at the University of California, Berkeley, in 1969, only one was a woman and she lectured in Oriental Art History. Margaret Peterson had taught painting at Berkeley from 1928 to 1950.

35. Ibid., 71, 74.

36. "Interview with Miriam Schapiro for the Women in the Arts in California Oral History Project," in East Hampton, N.Y., 10 September 1989, by Ruth Bowman, Archives of American Art, Smithsonian Institution, Southern California Research Center, San Marino, California. For the 1930s see "Leading Ladies," 156–78 and Nancy Acord, "Women of the WPA Art Projects: California Murals, 1933–1943," 1–36, both in *Yesterday and Tomorrow*, ed. Moore.

37. June Wayne, "The Male Artist as Stereotypical Female," Art Journal, College Art Association, summer 1973, reprinted in California Commission on the Status of Women, *Women in the Visual Arts*, 76–83.

38. Faith Wilding, "The Feminist Art Movement Southern California Style, 1970–1980," in *Yesterday and Tomorrow*, ed. Moore, 341–55.

39. Ibid., 344–45; Judy Chicago, *Through the Flower: My Struggle as a Woman Artist* (New York: Doubleday, 1975); "Interview with Sharon Share," by Kenon Breazeale, 5–6 September 1985, Double x oral history project, Archives of American Art, Smithsonian Institution, Southern California Research Center, 3.

40. Betty Ann Brown, "Autobiographical Imagery in the Art of Los Angeles Women," in *Yesterday and Tomorrow*, ed. Moore, 119–43.

41. "Interview with Miriam Schapiro," by Ruth Bowman, 6; "Interview with Connie Jenkins," by Kenon Breazeale, 13 March 1986, Double x oral history project, Archives of American Art, Smithsonian Institution, Southern California Research Center, 2, 6; and Miriam Schapiro, "Recalling Womanhouse," in *Yesterday and Tomorrow*, ed. Moore, 355–61.

42. Wilding, "The Feminist Art Movement Southern California Style," in *Yesterday and Tomorrow*, ed. Moore, 345–47.

43. Ibid.; Kirsten Grimstad, "Crysalis: A Magazine of Women's Culture," 369–72, in *Yesterday and Tomorrow*, ed. Moore.

44. Rita Cummings Belle, "Judy Chicago: The Dinner Party and the Birth Project," in *Yesterday and Tomorrow*, ed. Moore, 362; Riane Eisler, "Sex, Art, and Archetypes," *Women's Review of Books* 8.6 (March 1991): 16; Anne Marie Pois, "Review of The Dinner Party," in *Frontiers* 4.2 (1979): 72–76; and Judy Chicago, *The Dinner Party: A Symbol of Our Heritage* (New York: Anchor Press, Doubleday, 1979). Also see the essays in *Woman's Art Journal* 1.2 (fall 1980–winter 1981): 30–37.

45. Lucy R. Lippard, "More Alternate Spaces: The Woman's Building," *Art in America* 62 (May–June 1974): 85–86.

46. See especially Lucy Lippard, *Mixed Blessings: New Art in a Multicultural America* (New York: Pantheon, 1990).

5: With These Words

1. Laura Coltelli, *Winged Words: American Indian Writers Speak* (Lincoln: University of Nebraska Press, 1990), 72, 80.

2. Olsen, *Silences*, 33. The essays were originally published between 1965 and 1978.

3. Ibid., 146.

4. Coltelli, *Winged Words*. See especially the comments by Paula Gunn Allen, 135; Wendy Rose, 124; and Leslie Marmon Silko, 144, on their difficulties in developing this academic literary tradition.

5. More detailed descriptions may be in the unpublished records of anthropologists. I use only published accounts in my analysis here.

6. Elizabeth A. Brandt, On Secrecy and the Control of Knowledge: Taos Pueblo (New York: Human Sciences Press, 1980), 123–46.

7. Jay Miller, ed., Mourning Dove: A Salishan Autobiography (Lincoln: University of Nebraska Press, 1990); Gretchen M. Bataille and Kathleen Mullen Sands, American Indian Women: Telling Their Lives (Lincoln: University of Nebraska Press, 1984), 49–68; and Carolyn Gilman and Mary Jane Schneider, The Way to Independence: Memories of a Hidatsa Indian Family, 1840–1920 (St. Paul: Minnesota Historical Society Press, 1987).

8. Schneider, The Way to Independence, 2, 274.

9. Ibid., 285–87, 289, 344–47.

10. Lucy Thompson [Che-na-wah Weitch- ah-wah], To the American Indian: Reminiscences of a Yurok Woman (Berkeley: Heyday Books, 1991; reprint of 1916 edition).

11. Thompson, To the American Indian, 184. See also Peter E. Palmquist, With Nature's Children: Emma B. Freeman [1880–1928]—Camera and Brush (Eureka: Interface California Corporation, 1976), 47–48.

12. Miller, Mourning Dove, xxiii.

13. Ibid., 4, 78–79, 186.

14. Ibid., xvii, xx–xxi.

15. Hum-ishua [Mourning Dove], Cogewea: The Half-Blood (Lincoln: University of Nebraska Press, 1981; reprint of 1927 edition); letters dated July 1919 and 8 June 1930 are quoted in the introduction by Dexter Fisher, vii.

16. Ibid., 41, 120–30, 165.

17. Bataille and Sands, American Indian Women, 49–68.

18. Colson, Autobiographies of Three Pomo Women, 112–13, 137. Lucy Young, a member of the Lassik tribe of northern California told her story to Edith Van Allen Murphey in 1936, but it was not published until 1978 in the California Historical Society Quarterly. See No Rooms of Their Own: Women Writers of Early California, ed. Ida Rae Egli (Berkeley: Heyday Books, 1992), 47–58.

19. Charmian Kittredge London, The Log of the Snark (New York: Macmillan, 1915).

20. See especially, Marilyn Strathern, "Out of Context: The Persuasive Fictions of Anthropology," in Modernist Anthropology: From Fieldwork to Text, ed. Marc Manganaro (Princeton: Princeton University Press, 1990), 80–125.

21. Ute Gacs, Aisha Khan, Jerrie McIntyre, and Ruth Weinberg, eds., Women Anthropologists: Selected Biographies (Urbana: University of Illinois Press, 1989), contains information on most of the formally trained or professional anthropologists who wrote about the West. The broader view of women as anthropologists is in Nancy J. Parezo, "Anthropology: The Welcoming Silence," in Hidden Scholars: Women Anthropologists and the Native American Southwest, ed. Nancy J. Parezo (Albuquerque: University of New Mexico Press, 1993), 3–37.

22. Mary B. Watkins to Grace Nicholson, undated, "Fiesta of the Dead"; Mary B. Watkins to Grace Nicholson, 27 September 1909, Box 11; Evaline Nelson to Grace Nicholson, 20 March 1916, Box 6, Grace Nicholson Papers, Huntington Library, San Marino, California.

23. Constance DuBois is not included in Gacs, et al. Women Anthropologists. Some

biographical information is in Constance Goddard DuBois, "The Religion of the Luiseno Indians of Southern California," *University of California Publications in American Archaeology and Ethnology* 8.3 (1908): 70–72.

24. Emma Reh, *Navajo Consumption Habits*, ed. Terry R. Reynolds, University Museum, Occasional Papers, no. 9 (Las Cruces: New Mexico State University, 1983), 1–4. Reynolds says she was listed as the senior author on the article and that D'Arcy McNickle insisted in a private letter she was the senior author. Nevertheless, the article appeared as D'Arcy McNickle, "Peyote and the Indian," *Scientific Monthly* 57 (1943): 220–29.

25. Margaret M. Caffrey, *Ruth Benedict: Stranger in This Land* (Austin: University of Texas Press, 1989), 270.

26. See Barbara Babcock, "Taking Liberties, Writing from the Margins, and Doing It with a Difference," *Journal of American Folklore* 100 (1987): 390–411; Katherine Dunham, *Journey to Accompang* (New York: Henry Holt, 1946); and Deborah Gordon, "The Politics of Ethnographic Authority: Race and Writing in the Ethnography of Margaret Mead and Zora Neale Hurston," in *Modernist Anthropology*, ed. Manganaro, 162.

27. Ruth Leah Bunzel, *The Pueblo Potter: A Study of Creative Imagination in Primitive Art* (New York: Columbia University Press, 1929). See also Gacs, et al., *Women Anthropologists*, 31 for her interest in psychology. Gladys Reichard may seem an exception. In *Spider Woman: A Story of Navajo Weavers and Chanters* (New York: Macmillan, 1934) she recounted four summers spent near Ganado, Arizona, living with a Navajo family and learning to weave. Yet she too emphasized traditional culture and deemphasized the ways in which Navajos were confronting change. See Richard White, *The Roots of Dependency: Subsistence, Environment, and Social Change among the Choctaws, Pawnees, and Navajos* (Lincoln: University of Nebraska Press, 1983).

28. Ester S. Goldfrank, *Notes on an Undirected Life: As One Anthropologist Tells It*, Queen's College Publications in Anthropology, no. 3 (Flushing: Queens College Press, 1978), 43–60, 67–70.

29. Ibid., 80–86, 96.

30. Johannes Fabian, *Time and the Other: How Anthropology Makes Its Object* (New York: Columbia University Press, 1983), 47–52.

31. Ibid., 87–88. According to Burt A. Folkart, "Writer, Discovered at 80, Dies at 87," *Los Angeles Times*, 10 August 1983, p. 22, a UCLA anthropology professor discouraged Carobeth Laird from publishing *The Chemehuevis* (Banning, Calif.: Malki Museum Press, 1976). See also Carobeth Laird, *Encounter with an Angry God: My Life with John Peabody Harrington* (Banning, Calif.: Malki Museum Press, 1975).

32. Fabian, *Time and the Other*, 98, 117–19, 156–57.

33. Egli, *No Rooms of Their Own*, 2–3. Royce wrote her diary in 1849; she revised and edited it in 1878. Her son published it in 1932. See also Ralph Gabriel, "Concerning the Manuscript of Sarah Royce," in Sarah Royce, *A Frontier Lady* (Lincoln: University of Nebraska Press, 1977). Georgiana Kirby's autobiography, a formalized version of her diary, was published in 1889, the year of her death, but the original diary was apparently first published in part in 1992, in Egli, *No Rooms of Their Own*, 178.

34. *The Yellow Wallpaper* and the 1913 article "Why I Wrote 'The Yellow Wallpaper'" are both reprinted in *The Charlotte Perkins Gilman Reader,* edited and with an introduction by Ann J. Lane (New York: Pantheon, 1980), 3–20. Shari Benstock, *Women of the Left Bank: Paris, 1900–1940* (Austin: University of Texas Press, 1986), describes the coding even of women authors who left the United States to be more free to write. See especially the section on Gertrude Stein, 143–93.

35. Anne Ellis, *The Life of an Ordinary Woman* (New York: Houghton Mifflin, 1990; reprint of 1929 edition), 6.

36. Anne Ellis, *Plain Anne Ellis* (Lincoln: University of Nebraska Press, 1984; reprint of 1931 edition), 205, 207.

37. Ellis, *Life of an Ordinary Woman,* 237.

38. Ellis, *Plain Anne Ellis,* 208.

39. Ibid., 208–11.

40. Ibid., 235.

41. Ibid., 244–47.

42. Ibid., 262, 91–92.

43. Anne Ellis, *Sunshine Preferred,* 220, 235–36.

44. There is little biographical information published on Ellis. Elliott West in foreword to Anne Ellis, *The Life of an Ordinary Woman* (Lincoln: Bison Books, 1980), ix–xviii; and Anne Matlock, "'The Spirit of Anne Ellis," *Colorado Quarterly* 4.1 (summer 1955): 61–72 add very little to her own books. Matlock, who knew Ellis, did say a fourth book, *White Bread,* was rejected and never published.

45. Amy Ling, *Between Worlds: Women Writers of Chinese Ancestry* (New York: Pergamon, 1990), 21–55; and "Creating One's Self: The Eaton Sisters," in Shirley Geok-lin Lim and Amy Ling, *Reading the Literatures of Asian America* (Philadelphia: Temple University Press, 1992), 305–18.

46. Valerie Matsumoto, "Desperately Seeking 'Deirdre': Gender Roles, Multicultural Relations, and Nisei Women Writers of the 1930s," *Frontiers* 12.1 (1991): 19–32.

47. Tey Diana Rebolledo and Eliana S. Rivero, eds., *Infinite Divisions: An Anthology of Chicana Literature* (Tucson: University of Arizona Press, 1993), 16–19; Tey Diana Rebolledo, *Nuestras Mujeres: Hispanas of New Mexico: Their Images and Their Lives, 1582–1992* (Albuquerque: El Norte Publications/Academia, 1992), 38–39, 42–46; Tey Diana Rebolledo, "Narrative Strategies of Resistance in Hispana Writing," *The Journal of Narrative Technique* 20.2 (1990): 134–46; and Mary Helen Ponce, *The Lives and Works of Five Hispanic New Mexican Women Writers, 1878–1991* (Albuquerque: Southwest Hispanic Research Institute Working Papers, no. 119, summer 1992). See also Raymund A. Paredes, "The Evolution of Chicano Literature," in *Three American Literatures: Essays in Chicano, Native American, and Asian American Literature for Teachers of American Literature,* ed. Houston A. Baker Jr. (New York: Modern Language Association, 1982), 49–55.

48. Janice R. MacKinnon and Stephen R. MacKinnon, *Agnes Smedley: The Life and Times of an American Radical* (Berkeley: University of California Press, 1988), 82–132, discusses the writing and publishing of the book.

49. I have used the Feminist Press reprint of *Daughter of Earth*. For the friend's warning see MacKinnon and MacKinnon, *Agnes Smedley*, 115. For an analysis of Smedley and the proletarian realism movement see Paula Rabinowitz, *Labor and Desire: Women's Revolutionary Fiction in Depression America* (Chapel Hill: University of North Carolina Press, 1991), 10–12; and Deborah S. Rosenfelt, "Divided against Herself," *Moving On* 4 (April–May 1980): 15–23.

50. Information on publication is from Janice MacKinnon and Feminist Press, which reprinted *Daughter of Earth* in 1973 and 1986.

6: From the Borderlands

1. Anzaldúa, *Borderlands/La Frontera*, 195.

2. Ibid., 77, 82.

3. Frances A. Yates, *The Art of Memory* (Chicago: University of Chicago Press, 1966), especially 1–21, 371–86.

4. I am always astonished, although I should not be, at the number of injuries to women that students learn about through their family histories.

5. Fred Davis, *Yearning for Yesterday: A Sociology of Nostalgia* (New York: Free Press, 1979), 10, 15.

6. Ibid., 95.

7. Ibid., 33–35.

8. Ibid., 116.

9. Rita Felski, "Feminism, Postmodern-ism, and the Critique of Modernity," *Cultural Critique*, no. 13 (fall 1989): 48.

10. John Mack Faragher, "Gunslingers and Bureaucrats," *New Republic*, 14 December 1992, 29–36; and William H. Truettner and Alexander Nemerov, "More Bark Than Bite: Thoughts on the Traditional—and Not Very Historical—Approach to Western Art," *Journal of Arizona History* 33 (autumn 1992): 311–24.

11. William Truettner, *The West as America* (Washington, D.C.: Museum of American Art, Smithsonian Institution, 1991).

12. Goetzmann and Goetzmann, *The West of the Imagination*, xv–xviii. See also Corlann Bush, "The Way We Weren't: Images of Women and Men in Cowboy Art," in *The Women's West*, ed. Susan Armitage and Elizabeth Jameson, (Norman: University of Oklahoma Press, 1987), 19–34.

13. "Time to Circle the Wagons," *Newsweek*, 24 June 1991, 70.

14. For women's history see Elizabeth Jameson, "Toward a Multicultural History of Women in the Western United States," *Signs* 13.4 (1988): 761–91; and Susan Armitage, "Women and Men in Western History: A Stereotypical Vision," *Western Historical Quarterly* 15.4 (1985): 380–95. Patricia Nelson Limerick, *Trails: Toward a New Western History* (Lawrence: University Press of Kansas, 1991) contains a sampling of different topics. The debate can be followed in Gerald D. Nash, "Point of View: One Hundred Years of Western History," *Journal of the West* 32.1 (January 1993): 3–4; Susan Armitage, Elizabeth

Jameson, and Joan M. Jensen, "A Western Forum Response: The New Western History, Another Perspective," *Journal of Western History* 32.3 (July 1993): 5–6; and Howard N. Rabinowitz, "The New Western History Goes to Town, or Don't Forget That Your Urban Hamburger Was Once a Rural Cow: A Review Essay," *Montana* 43.2 (spring 1993): 73–77.

15. Larry McMurtry, "How the West Was Won or Lost," *New Republic*, 22 October 1990, 32.

16. Christine Battersby, *Gender and Genius: Toward a Feminist Aesthetics* (Bloomington: Indiana University Press, 1989). See also Price, *Primitive Art in Civilized Places*; and the introduction in *Feminism/Postmodern-ism*, ed. Linda J. Nicholson (New York: Routledge, 1989), 1–5.

17. Linda Hutcheon, *The Politics of Postmodernism* (New York: Routledge, 1989), 162–68.

18. Naomi Schor, *Reading in Detail: Aesthetics and the Feminine* (New York: Routledge, 1989; reprint of 1987 edition).

19. Lang and Lang, *Etched in Memory*, 319, 331.

20. Randy Rosen and Catherine C. Brawer, curators, *Making Their Mark: Women Artists Move into the Mainstream, 1970–1985* (New York: Abbeville, 1989).

21. Hilde Hein, "The Role of Feminist Aesthetics in Feminist Theory," *Journal of Aesthetics and Art Criticism* 48.4 (fall 1990): 281–91.

22. Anita Silvers, "Has Her(oine's) Time Now Come?" *Journal of Aesthetics and Art Criticism* 48.4 (fall 1990): 370.

23. Hutcheon, *Politics of Postmodernism*, 141–68.

24. Lucy R. Lippard, *From the Center: Feminist Essays on Women's Art* (New York: Dutton, 1976), 2, 8, 11.

25. Lippard, *Mixed Blessings*, 6, 17.

26. I have drawn heavily on Hutcheon, *The Politics of Postmodernism*, and Nicholson, *Feminism/Postmodernism*, for this section.

27. Jane Caplan, "Postmodernism, Poststructuralism, and Deconstruction: Notes for Historians," *Contemporary European History* 22 (S–D 1989): 260–78.

28. Ibid.

29. Hutcheon, *Politics of Postmodernism*, 143–60.

30. Nicholson, introduction to *Feminism/Postmodernism*, 6–11.

31. Nina Baym, "The Madwoman and Her Languages: Why I Don't Do Feminist Theory," in *Feminist Issues in Literary Scholarship*, ed. Shari Benstock, (Bloomington: University of Indiana Press, 1987), 45–61. The essay originally appeared in vol. 3 (1984–85) of the Tulsa Studies in Women's Literature. See also Tey Diana Rebolledo, "The Politics of Poetics: Or, What Am I, A Critic, Doing in This Text Anyhow?" 346–55, and Norma Alarcón, "The Theoretical Subject(s) of This Bridge Called My Back and Anglo-American Feminism," 356–67, both in Anzaldúa, *Making Face, Making Soul*.

32. Trinh T. Minh-ha, "Not You/Like You: Post-Colonial Women and the Inter-locking Questions of Identity and Difference," 371–75; Gloria Anzaldúa, "La Consciencia de la Mestiza/Toward a New Consciousness," 377–89; Maria Lugones, "Playfulness, 'World'-Traveling, and Loving Perception," 390–402; and Barbara Christian, "The Race for Theory," 335–45, all in Anzaldúa, *Making Face, Making Soul*.

33. bell hooks, *Talking Back: thinking feminist, thinking black* (Boston: South End Press, 1989), 35–41.

34. Trinh T. Minh-ha, "Cotton and Iron," in *Out There: Marginalization and Contemporary Cultures*, ed. Russell Ferguson, Martha Gever, Trinh T. Minh-ha, and Cornel West (Cambridge: MIT Press, 1990), 327–37.

35. Hutcheon, *Politics of Postmodernism*, 163–68.

INDEX

Abiquiu, New Mexico, 75
abstraction, 149
Achey, Mary Elizabeth Michael, 46
African Americans, 22, 90, 91, 96, 118
Akins, Zoë, 60, 76–78, 80, 92, 121, 133
Alarcón, Norma, 148
Albers, Josef, 96
Albuquerque, New Mexico, 43, 69, 121
Allan, Maud, 89, 91
Allen, Elsie, 63, 84, 86
Allen, Paula Gunn, 32
anthropology, storytelling and, 109,
    111, 114–16; women in, 116–20,
    128
Anzaldúa, Gloria, 34, 131, 145, 148
Armstrong, Julia, and Royce
    Armstrong, 123
art, a definition for, 100; abstract
    expressionist, 93; assemblage art,
    96; brokers for, 79; canon and
    exemplary, 142; children in, 50–
    51; craft and, 140; detail and ideal
    in, 141; documenting, 96, 98;
    domestic, 29; healing and, 29;
    Hispanic, 70; Indian art as
    primitive, 80; interpreting western
    art, 135; life reconciled to, 20, 33;
    meanings for, 40; men and, 93–95;
    modern, 66, 93; nostalgia and
    success in, 133; participatory, 103;
    public, 28; reputation in, 141;

schools for, 45; validation through,
    30, 97; women in, 31, 45, 80, 143
"Art and Technology," 97
Art Association, San Francisco, 46
Arzner, Dorothy, 76
Asian Americans, 124
Atchison, Topeka, and Santa Fe
    Railway, 60; as Santa Fe Railroad,
    43, 70
Atherton, Gertrude, 121
audience, building the, 101; community
    as, 103; finding new, 144; taming of,
    86; the listening, 107; the native, 86,
    113; the urban, 129
Austin, Mary, 60, 67–73, 79, 80, 82,
    121, 123, 129
Autobiography of a Papago Woman
    (Underhill), 118
Azawa, Ruth, 96

B

Baca, Judy, 28–32
Bacchanal, the, 22
Back to Her Tribe, Hudson, 40
Baker, Josephine, 91
ballet, 92
bargaining, 62
Barnard College, 21
Barrego, Mary, 123
Basketmaker, the, 15–17
basketry, 16, 38, 42, 43, 56, 59, 62, 80, 81

Baym, Nina, 148
beading, 86
Bear Woman (Hudson), 51
beat movement, the, 93
Beaty, Joan, 95
Beloved House, the, 69
Benedict, Ruth, 116, 117, 119
Benson, Mary, 63
Berkeley, California, 22
Berlin, Germany, 89
Billop, Camille, 96
Billy, Susan, 84–85, 102
Black Art, 96
Black Mountain College, 96
"Blessing," Hogan, 107
Boaz, Franz, 117
Bobbs Merrill, 68, 71
Body/Culture: Chicano Figuration
    (Baca), 28
Bole-maru, the, 88
Boorstin, Daniel, 136
Booth, William, 67
borderlands, cultural, 120
Borderlands, Anzaldúa, 131
Boston Symphony, 89
Bretteville, Sheila de, 100
Brigman, Annie W., 52
Brodt, Helen Tanner, 46
Brown, Joan, 95, 96
"The Bu-ta-Madtha," 51
Buffalo Bird Woman, 110
Bunzel, Ruth, 118
burial and basketry, 39, 41–42
Burke, Annie, 84
burlesque, 90
By Our Own Hands, 98

C

Cabeza de Baca, Fabiola, 70, 124–25
Cadenasso, Giuseppe, 53
California, 38, 52, 68, 76, 88–89, 94–
    96, 110
California Commission on the Status
    of Women, 97
California Institute for the Arts, 98, 100
California School of Design, 45
California School of Fine Arts

(CSFA), 94–95
California State University, Fresno,
    99–100
Call, the, 125
capitalism, 136
Caplan, Jane, 146–47
Carlisle Indian School, 55
Carmel, California, 52
Carpenter, Grace, 44. See also
    Hudson, Grace
Carpenter, Helen, 44
Cassidy, Inez, 121–23
Cattle (Eaton), 124
Chain, Helen Henderson, 46
Che-na-wah Weitch-ah-wah, 111
Chemehuevi, the, 120
Chicago, Illinois, 46, 101
Chicago, Judy, 31, 99–101
Chicago Field Museum, 49
Chicago World's Fair, 90
Chicano/a, 31. See also Mexican-
    American, Hispanic
Chicano Art Movement, 30
Chickasaw, the, 107
Chimayo, New Mexico, 70
China, 125
Chinese, the, 25, 124, 125
Chona, Maria, 114
Choreopoet, the, 20–24
choreopoetry, 22
Christian, Barbara, 149
Cochiti (Pueblo), 119
Cogewea (Quintasket), 110, 113
colcha, 70
collecting, 61–62
colonialism, 37, 102
Colorado, 121–23
Colorado River, 71
Colson, Elizabeth, 114
Columbia University, 117
Colville Reservation, 112
Commissioner of Indian Affairs, 87
"Common Woman Poems, The,"
    Grahn, 21
*Complexity and Contradiction in
    Architecture* (Venturi), 6
Cotton Club, Harlem, 91

counterculture, the, 93
Crabtree, Lotta, 88
creativity, 60, 108
critics, 95, 97
crochet, 70
Crothers, Rachel, 76
Crysalis, 98, 101
culture, borders/divides of, 34, 39, 119, 144; documenting, 110–11; historical memory of, 82, 131–32; maintaining/preserving, 61, 109–19, 132, 139; privileged position of artifacts in, 85; transmitting, 108–10; women as cultural workers, 131–38
Cunningham, Imogen, 52

D

Dakota, the, 117
dance, American, 34, 91, 92; community, 87–89; concert, 89–91; Haitian, 118; Indian, 111; modern, 90–93; troupe, 21, 90
Dancer, the, 17–20
dau, the, 16, 17, 32, 40, 102
Daughter of Earth (Smedley), 125, 127
Daughters of the American Revolution, 69
Davis, Fred, 133, 134
Death and Life of American Cities, The (Jacobs), 6
deconstruction, 34, 147
Del Rio, Dolores, 90–91
Deloria, Ella Cara, 117
deMille, Agnes, 92–93, 133
demonstrations, 43, 56. *See also* teaching
Densmore, Frances, 114
Denver, Colorado, 53
Depression, the, 75; the Great Depression, 60, 66
diaries, 120
Diaz, Isabel, 119
Dick, Jeff, 43
Dick, Joseppa, 38, 40, 42–44, 51, 63, 147
Didion, Joan, cited, 8
Dinner Party, The (Chicago) 31, 98,

101, 141
distribution, the industry of, 87
Dodge, Kathleen Carman, 123
double x, the gallery, 98, 101
DuBois, Constance, 116, 117
Duncan, Isadora, 3, 17–18, 34, 71, 89, 91, 92, 103
Dunham, Katherine, 91, 118
Durieux, Tilla, 126

E

Eaton, Edith, 124
Eaton, Winnifred, 124
Echo, California, 42
Eckerman, Margaret, 118
education, feminist, 99
Eel River, 64
1893 Exposition, 46
Ellis, Anne, 69, 121–23
employment, art as, 39
Encounter with an Angry God (Laird), 119
Espinosa, Carmen Gertrudis, 124
ethnographer, 110
Eureka, California, 52, 53, 111
Europe, 17, 18, 86, 88, 89, 145
Everyman's Genius (Austin), 68, 71
"Everywoman," the play, 55
exhibiting, 45, 46, 51, 66, 84, 97. See also galleries
Experiences Facing Death, (Austin), 71

F

Fabian, Johannes, 119, 120
Falkenstein, Claire, 96
feminism, 140–50
Feminist Art Program, 99–100
Feminist Press, 127
Feminist Studio Workshop (FSW), 101
Field Columbian Museum, Chicago, 64
Foote, Mary Hallock, 46
for colored girls who have considered suicide/when the rainbow is enuf (Shange), 21
Ford, The (Austin), 67
Forum, The, 72–73
Frankfurter Zeitung, The, 126

Fred Harvey Company, 60
Freeman, Edwin, 53
Freeman, Emma, 38, 52–53, 133
Freeman Art Company, 55
Fresno, California, 99–100
Fuller, Loie, 18

G

galleries, 30, 51, 98, 100. *See also*
    exhibiting
gender, 34, 88, 124, 134, 139–40, 142.
    See also sexuality
genius, 139–40
Germany, 125
Gerowitz, Judy, 99
Ghost Dances, 87–88
Ghost Ranch, 75, 76
Gilman, Charlotte Perkins, 121
Gilpin, Laura, 52
Goetzmann, William H., and William
    N. Goetzmann, 86, 135
Goldfrank, Esther, 118–19
Goldman, Emma, 125
Good Bird, 110
Gordon, Deborah, 118
Gordon-Cumming, Constance
    Frederica, 46
Grace Hudson Museum, 52
Graham, George, Dr., 90
Graham, Martha, 90, 92, 133
Grahn, Judy, 21
Grandmothers of the Light (Allen), 32
Great Depression, the, 60, 66, 75
Great Wall, The, 31
Green, Rayna, 64
Green Fountains, 78
Greenslet, Ferris, 68, 71
Guie, Heister Dean, 112

H

Halprin, Ann, 154 n 7
Hansberry, Lorraine, 76
Harrington, John Peabody, 120
Harvard University, 117
Harvey, Fred, 43
Hatch-Billops Collection, 96
Hawaii, 24, 48, 49

healing, 29, 32
Hearst, Phoebe, 117
Hein, Hilde, 142
Hellman, Lillian, 76
Henshaw, Henry, 43
Hidatsu, the, 110
highways, 60
Hispanics, 70; Mexican Americans, 90;
    Chicano/a, 31
historiography, 135
history, 33–34, 82, 137–39, 143–46;
    women in, 136 n 4
Hogan, Linda, cited, 107
hooks, bell, 34, 149
Hoopa, the, 52
Houghton Mifflin, 67, 68, 71, 123
Howland, H. H., 68
Hudson, Grace, 16–17, 38, 40, 44,
    66, 133
Hudson, John, 16–17, 40, 46–49, 61–62
humanity, becoming/becoming
    conscious of, 17, 31, 32
Humboldt Bay, 53
Humboldt County, 52
Hupa, the, 64
Hurston, Zora Neal, 118
Hyde, Helen, 160 n 55

I

Indian Art of the United States, exhibit, 67
Indian Detours, 60
Indianapolis, Indiana, 68
Indians, 109; Native Americans, 38,
    52, 57

J

Jacobs, Jane, 6
Japanese, nisei, 124
Jaramillo, Cleofas, 70, 124
Johnson, Jennie Day, 118–19

K

Katum, 51
Kauser, Alice, 78
Keatinge, Mary Alice, 52
"The Ki-me-ya," 51
Kingston, Maxine Hong, 24–28

Kitt Peak, 59, 81
"The Kol-pi-ta," 51
Korean War, 95
Kroeber, Alfred, 111, 117

L

La Casa Querida, 69
Laguna (Pueblo), 118–19
Laird, Carobeth, 119, 120
Laird, George, 120
Land of Little Rain (Austin), 67
Lands of the Sun, The (Austin), 68
Lang, Gladys, and Kurt Lang, 141
Lange, Dorothea, 52
Lassik, the, 164 n 18
Lea, Aurora Lucero-White, 70, 124
Leach, Henry Goddard, 73
Levine, Lawrence, 85–86
Lewis, Samella, 96
Life, 93
Life of an Ordinary Woman, The (Ellis),
    121
Lincoln, Dalottiwa, 110
Lincoln, Harry, 110
Lippard, Lucy, 102, 143–45
Literary Guild, 71
literary-artists, 71, 76, 118–25
lithographer, 95, 97
London, Charmian, 115
London, England, 48, 93
London, Jack, 115
Lonesome Dove (McMurtry), 137
Los Angeles, California, 76, 90, 96
Los Angeles Council of Women Artists
    (LACWA), 97
Los Angeles County Museum, 97
Lotz, Matilda, 46
Lucero-White (Lea), Aurora, 70, 124
Lugones, Maria, 148
Luhan, Mabel Dodge, 74
Luhan, Tony, 74
Lundebert, Helen, 96

M

MacAgy, Douglas, 94
McBride, Henry, 75
McCann, Coward, 127

MacKinnon, Janice, and Stephen
    MacKinnon, 127
McMurtry, Larry, 137
Madonna of the Trail, 69
Making Their Mark, 142
marginalization, 108
marketing, 38, 42, 48, 59–82, 96, 97
marriage, 18–20, 27, 30, 46–50, 53, 55,
    57, 74, 78
maru, the, 88
Mason Opera House, 90
Maxidiwiac, 110, 111
Mechanic's Fair, 46
memory, 132–33, 141
Mendocino, California, 4
Mendocino County, 40, 44
Mendoza, Lydia, 91
Mesa Grande, the, 116
Mescalero Apache, the, 87
Mesquakie, the, 110
Mesquakie-Winnebago, the, 110
Metropolitan Opera House, 89
Mewhinney, John, 51
Mexican Americans, 90; Hispanics, 70,
    Chicano/a, 31
Mexico, 29, 90, 131
Michaelis, Karin, 126
Michelson, Truman, 110
Mills, C. Wright, 6
Minh-ha, Trinh, 145, 148
Mitchell, Tom, 51
Mixed Blessings: New Art in a
    Multicultural America (Lippard), 144
Mock, Ed, 21
modernism, 6–8, 93, 99, 140, 143, 149–50
Montez, Lola, 90
Muralista, the, 28–32
murals, 31
Museum of African American Art, 96
Museum of Modern Art, 67, 75, 80
Museum of Modern Art,
    San Francisco, 101
museums for art, 94
music, 91, 93
My Life (Duncan), 17
myths, creating, 131, 134

N

National Book Critics Circle, 24
Native Americans, 38, 52, 57; Indians,
109. *See also* separately by tribe
Navajo, the, 16, 117
Nelson, Evaline, 116
New Deal, the, 66
New Mexico, 40, 64, 69–72, 73, 87,
115, 124–25
New Western History, the, (NWH),
135–37
New York, 22, 48, 67, 75, 76, 78, 82,
91–96 passim, 100, 102, 122, 125
New York Art Students' League, 45
New York Symphony, 89
Nicholson, Grace, 61–64, 66, 116
Norman, Dorothy, 74
Northridge, California, 30
nostalgia, 132–34
nudes, studies of, 52

O

Oakland, California, 18, 124
Oakland Museum of Art, 97
Oberlin College, 117
O'Keeffe, Georgia, 60, 73–76, 79, 80
Oklahoma! (deMille), 93
Old Hawaiian Woman (Hudson,) 50
Old Maid, The (Akins), 60
Olsen, Tillie, 8, 83, 103, 108
Omaha, Nebraska, 108
O'Neal, Lila, 117
oral traditions, 25, 132
Orleans, California, 116
Oroville, California, 122
Osumari, Halifu, 21
Otero-Warren, Nina, 70, 124
Owl Woman, 114
Oyama, Mary, 124

P

Pacific Commercial Advertiser, 49
painting, 38–46, 51, 73, 96
Paiute, the, 16
Palmquist, Peter, 52
Papinta, 90
Parezo, Nancy J., 116

Paris Exposition, 48
Parrish, Essie, 88
Pasadena, California, 61, 76, 96
Pasadena Art Institute, 64
Pasadena Playhouse, The, 76
Patterns of Culture, Benedict, 116
Perkins, Lucy Fitch, 123
Peters, Rosa, 51
photography, 38, 43, 45, 52–53, 85–86
Pinto, Charlie, 42
Pinto, Mary, 43, 51
placayasos, 31
playwrights, 76
poetry, 21–22
politics, 113, 123, 126
Pomo, the, 15, 16, 38, 40, 42–44, 46,
48, 50, 61, 63, 81, 84, 102–3, 114
Pomo, the Kashaya, 88
portraiture, 51, 55
postcolonialism, 136, 145
postmodernism, 6–7, 8–10, 83–104,
102, 143–49, 153
poststructuralism, 146
Potter Valley, 44
pottery, 86, 96
Poway, California, 120
presentism, 145
Press Club, San Francisco, 46
Primavera (Botticelli), 19
Public Broadcasting, 135
Pueblo Indians, 70

Q

Quail Woman, 15–17, 40
Quakers, the, 96
Quintasket, Christine, 110, 112–14

R

race, 28, 34, 124
Raven, Arlene, 100
reality, social, 150; theories of, 146–47
Rebolledo, Tey Diana, 148
regionalism, 66
Reh, Emma, 117
religion, 87
Richart, Emma, 52. *See also* Freeman,
Emma

Richmond, Virginia, 84
Rio Grande, 71
Rodeo (deMille), 92
Rodin, August, 18
romanticism, 121
Rumbold, Hugo, 78
Russian River, 42
Ruth St. Denis School of Dancing and
    Related Arts, 90
Ryan, Jimmy, 113

S

Saar, Betty, 96
Saguache County, 123
St. Denis, Ruth, 89–90, 91
St. Louis, Missouri, 20
St. Paul Farmer, the, 111
Salish, the, 112, 113
San Fernando Valley, 29, 31
San Francisco, California, 18, 21, 22,
    45, 46, 50, 53, 55, 56, 86, 88–90,
    94, 101, 108
San Joaquin Valley, 99
San Luis Valley, 122
Sanger, Margaret, 126
Santa Barbara, California, 90
Santa Clara Valley, 67
Santa Fe, New Mexico, 69, 72, 123
Santa Fe Railroad, 43, 60, 70
Sarah and Son (Akins),76
Saturday Review of Literature, 72
Sawyer, Raymond, 21
Schapiro, Miriam, 100
scholars, 131–34
Schor, Naomi, 141
Scripps College, 96
sculptor, 96
Seattle, Washington, 52
secrecy, cultural, 109, 119
self, creation of/sense of, 26, 29, 33–34,
    75; one's art as one's identity, 42;
    significant others, 57
Sergeant, Elizabeth Shepley, 72
sexuality, 18–20, 33, 55, 74, 79, 87, 91,
    101, 113, 128–29
Shange, Ntozake, 20–24
Silences (Olsen), 8, 83, 108

Silvers, Anita, 142
Sioux, the, 87
Smedley, Agnes, 125–27
Smith, Hassel, 94
Smithsonian (Institute), 46, 51–52,
    64, 84
Smithsonian Museum of American
    Art, 135, 136
Social and Public Art Resource Center
    (SPARC), 31
Soil Conservation Service, 117
songs, 114
Sonoma County, 42
Sonoma State College, 21
Sonoma State University, 28
Spivak, Gayatri, 33–34
Staempfli, George, 96
Stanislavsky, Konstantin, 19
Starry Adventure (Austin),72
Stein, Gertrude, 121
Stephenson, Matilda, 115
Stevens, Bertha, 56
Stieglitz, Alfred, 73–75
Stockton, California, 25
Storyteller, the, 24–28
storytelling, 25, 26, 33–34, 109–18,
    120–21, 127–29
studios, 43, 52, 78
Sui Sin Far, 124. *See also* Edith Eden
Sun House, 52
symbols for community, 31

T

Taos, New Mexico, 4, 74, 75
Taos Pueblo, 109
teaching, 18, 20, 21, 25, 40, 44, 84, 95,
    99, 110, 117
Teequalt, 112
Tempe, Arizona, 125
Their Eyes Were Watching God
    (Hurston), 118
Thompson, Bertha, 56, 111
Thompson, Lucy, 56, 110, 111–12
Thompson, Milton, 111
Thus Spake Zarathustra (Nietzsche), 17
To the American Indian (Thompson),
    111

Tohono O'odham, the, 59, 80–81, 114, 118
Toomer, Jean, 75
Toronto, Canada, 89
tourism, 60, 70; tourists, 52, 53
Toynbee, Arnold J., 6
traditionalism, 70
Trail Book, The (Austin), 67
Treiman, Joyce, 96
Trinity River, 64
Truettner, William, 135
Tucson, Arizona, 59
Tulere, the, 64

U

Ukiah, California, 42, 44, 46
Ukiah Valley, 63, 85
Underhill, Ruth, 114, 118
United States, 20, 89
University of California, Berkeley, 25, 117
University of California, Los Angeles, 21, 99
University of California, San Diego, 100
University of Chicago, 117
University of Hawaii, 25
University of Pennsylvania, 64

V

validation, 97, 124
Venturi, Robert, 6
Voyage of the Snark, London, 115

W

Waheenee: An Indian Girl's Story, Wilson, 111
Washington, 112, 113
Washington, D. C., 46
Watanna, Otono, 124. *See also* Winifred Eden
Watkins, Mary B., 116
Watson, James E., 68
Wayne, June, 95–96, 97
weaving, 70
Weltfish, Gene, 16
West, the, 3–6; cultural control over,

86; fantasizing, 52; marketing, 80; nostalgia and, 133, 136
West As America, The: Reinterpreting Images of America, 135
West of the Imagination, The (Goetzmann and Goetzmann), 135
westering, accounts of, 44
White, Edith, 46
Whitman, Walt, 3, 20
Whitney Museum, New York, 96
Wild West shows, 87
Williams, Paulette, 20
Wilson, Gilbert, 110–11
Wilson, Maude, 52
Woman Warrior, The (Kingston), 24, 25
Womanhouse, Los Angeles, 98, 100
Woman's Building, Los Angeles, 98, 101, 102
Womanspace gallery, 100
Women's Home Companion, 122
Women's Studies Program, Sonoma, 21
Wong, Jade Snow, 124
Wood, Beatrice, 96
Woolf, Virginia, cited, 37
Works Progress Administration (WPA), 96
World War I, 57, 109
World War II, 29, 94, 96, 116, 124, 140
writers, 70; women and writing, 108
writing, coding in, 121

Y

Yamamota, Hisaye, 124
Yellow Wallpaper, The (Gilman), 121
Yokayo, California, 40, 42–44
Yosemite, 46
Young, Lucy, 164 n 18
"Young America 1960," 96
Yurok, the, 52, 56, 110, 111–12